GILL'S
BAKES & CAKES
SIMPLE * QUICK * DELICIOUS

Gillian Cottell is a talented baker from Dublin. She attended culinary school and worked as a chef for over six years. During the pandemic, she recognised the need for resourceful baking guidance, and launched her own social media platform dedicated to making baking accessible to everyone. Now a trusted authority in the food-blogging community, her in-depth knowledge of ingredients, techniques and troubleshooting common baking pitfalls has become invaluable to both beginner enthusiasts and seasoned bakers alike.

gills_bakesandcakes

GILL'S
BAKES & CAKES
SIMPLE * QUICK * DELICIOUS

Gillian Cottell

THE O'BRIEN PRESS
DUBLIN

This book is dedicated to each and every follower who has supported me throughout the years: thank you for making this dream of mine become a reality.

First published 2024 by
The O'Brien Press Ltd,
12 Terenure Road East, Rathgar,
Dublin 6, D06 HD27, Ireland.
Tel: +353 1 4923333; Fax: +353 1 4922777
E-mail: books@obrien.ie
Website: obrien.ie
The O'Brien Press is a member of Publishing Ireland.

ISBN: 978-1-78849-443-4

8 7 6 5 4 3 2 1
28 27 26 25 24

Printed and bound by Drukarnia Skleniarz in Poland.
The paper in this book is produced using pulp from managed forests.

Published in:

CONTENTS

WELCOME

Welcome to the world of Gill's Bakes and Cakes! In 2019 I started a recipe blog on social media to share my love of baking and cooking, and now here we are with my first book. Thank you to all my followers who have supported me on this journey and who have helped to make my wildest dreams come true. I am over the moon to bring you this selection of my favourite bakes and cakes.

I'm a passionate foodie, looking to help people learn, grow and have fun in the kitchen. I like to share recipes that I truly love and to give you the confidence to create them yourself.

I grew up in a food-loving family and honed my skills in professional kitchens. As a dedicated self-taught home baker, I understand the joys and challenges of creating delicious treats from scratch. Through my social media presence and blog, I have been on a mission to demystify baking and inspire others to embrace their inner pastry chef in the comfort of their own kitchen. By providing easy-to-follow recipes and step-by-step instructions, I aim to make the magical world of baking accessible to all.

Within the pages of this cookbook, you will discover a delightful assortment of recipes that cater to all taste buds and skill levels. From classic cookies to beautiful celebration cakes that are a feast for the eyes and palate, each recipe is crafted with love and precision, ensuring your baking adventures are nothing short of extraordinary.

There are three levels to the recipes:

*   **Super simple**
* *   **Not too tricky**
* * * **Showstopper**

Whether you're a real home baker or a baking novice eager to learn the ropes, this book promises to be your ultimate guide to the world of baking. So, preheat your ovens, dust off your aprons and get ready to immerse yourself in the sheer joy of baking and, of course, eating your heavenly bakes. Let's bake, create and savour the sweetness of life, one delicious recipe at a time!

Enjoy x

BAKING ESSENTIALS

BAKING EQUIPMENT

This is a list of all of the baking equipment and tools I could not live without. I like to keep baking tins very simple, with no strange sizes or shapes. My favourite baking tin is definitely 20 x 20cm (8 x 8 inch) square tin: it is the ultimate traybake tin and suits a wide range of the recipes in this book, e.g. chocolate biscuit cakes, brownies, traybake cakes, to name a few.

TINS

20 x 20cm (8 x 8 inch) square tin – The ULTIMATE traybake tin!

20cm (8 inch) cake tin – A classic all-rounder for sponge cakes.

15cm (6 inch) cake tin – Great for stacked, tall celebration cakes.

Rectangular tin – For cinnamon rolls, bread and butter pudding, crumbles, this is your tin.

20cm (8 inch) springform tin – We all love cheesecake and this is the only tin to make a cheesecake in. Easy release is key.

900g (2 lb) loaf tin – I have a soft spot for loaf cakes: simple to make, easy to portion. This tin is definitely a staple.

2 flat baking trays or baking sheets – It goes without saying … COOKIES!

Muffin tray with 12 cups – I am pretty sure this was my first-ever baking tin when I was a kid. You can't have a baking collection without one – right?!

20cm (8 inch) circular tin or tart dish – Banoffee pie, apple pie, we all love pie. Probably not my most-used dish but 100 per cent I couldn't live without it.

TOOLS

Baking parchment – We can't be letting our cakes stick to the tin.

Bread knife – I always cut my layer cakes with one, as it gives you more control.

Cake scraper – Looking for a super-smooth iced cake? Gently heat a cake scraper in warm water, wipe it clean and then run it all along the outside of your cake for a flawless finish.

Chopping board – I think this one goes without saying.

Cupcake/muffin cases – Always good to keep these in stock.

Electric hand whisk or stand mixer – If I could have only one tool, it would have to be an electric hand whisk or a stand mixer. They incorporate air perfectly into your lovely bakes and make the fluffiest icings. They make kneading dough so much easier, too.

Grater – Zest, zest, zest! And the occasional carrot, too (for my delicious carrot cake recipe).

Hand whisk – Great for a quick mix of an egg wash or to mix dry ingredients evenly.

Ice-cream scoop – The best way to get evenly sized cupcakes, muffins or pancakes.

Measuring spoons – Get your salt and spice measurements exact.

Oven thermometer – All ovens fluctuate in temperature and can read wrong. Pop in an oven thermometer to get the oven's temperature exactly right.

Palette knife – The best tool for creating beautifully iced cakes.

Pastry brush – Essential for applying an egg wash to give a bright, shiny bake.

Piping bag – Grab yourself a reusable piping bag so you never are without one.

Piping nozzle – You can't live without a basic round nozzle or a star tip. Start with these and you'll be flying.

Rolling pin – Definitely essential but I won't lie: I have used the odd glass bottle before!

Round cookie cutter set – Cookies, scones … or you can use a glass or cup.

Rubber spatula – For scraping all that batter from your bowl with ease.

Ruler – Key for following recipes with dough that needs to be rolled out.

Sieve – This is something we all need, to avoid lumps in our cakes, to finish bakes with icing sugar or for straining jams.

Small measuring bowls – One of the first things I learned in culinary school was to prep by weighing out ingredients. Fail to prepare = Prepare to fail!

Weighing scales – Baking is an exact science – no measuring by eye!

Wire cooling rack – Nobody likes a soggy bottom! A cooling rack allows air to circulate all around your bakes as they cool down, for a perfect fresh bake.

Wooden spoons – Handy to have as they are super-versatile for every type of mix in the kitchen.

ESSENTIAL BAKING INGREDIENTS

These are the ingredients that I always have in my baking kit. No fancy ingredients – they are all simple ingredients you can pick up in any local supermarket and have a very long shelf life.

Baking powder

Basic colour food gels

Bicarbonate of soda/baking soda

Butter, salted and unsalted

Chocolate bars (milk, dark, white)

Chocolate chips (milk, dark, white)

Cocoa powder

Cornflour

Eggs

Flour: plain and self-raising flour

Food gels: a set of basic colours (red, blue, yellow)

Frozen fruit

Mixed nuts

Mixed sprinkles

Non-stick spray

Salt

Sugar: caster, dark brown & light brown sugar

Vanilla extract/vanilla pods/vanilla bean paste

CONVERSION TABLES

OVEN TEMPERATURES

°C	Fan °C	°F	Gas Mark
140°C	Fan 120°C	275°F	Gas 1
150°C	Fan 130°C	300°F	Gas 2
160°C	Fan 140°C	325°F	Gas 3
180°C	Fan 160°C	350°F	Gas 4
190°C	Fan 170°C	375°F	Gas 5
200°C	Fan 180°C	400°F	Gas 6
220°C	Fan 200°C	425°F	Gas 7
230°C	Fan 210°C	450°F	Gas 8
240°C	Fan 220°C	475°F	Gas 9

DRY WEIGHTS

10g	½ oz
25g	1 oz
50g	2 oz
75g	3 oz
110g	4 oz
150g	5 oz
175g	6 oz
200g	7 oz
225g	8 oz

LIQUID MEASUREMENTS

ml	fl
5ml	½ fl oz
30ml	1 fl oz
50ml	2 fl oz
75ml	3 fl oz
125ml	4 fl oz
150ml	5 fl oz
180ml	6 fl oz
200ml	7 fl oz
230ml	8 fl oz

USEFUL TIPS & TRICKS

MELTING CHOCOLATE

Bain-marie: The best way to melt chocolate is in a bain-marie. This will gently heat the chocolate and prevent it from burning. Half-fill a medium saucepan with water and place over a low heat with a heatproof bowl placed on top of the saucepan, making sure the bowl doesn't touch the water. Break the chocolate into small pieces and place them in the bowl. Stir occasionally until the chocolate is completely melted.

Microwave: Break the chocolate into small pieces and place them in a microwave-safe bowl. Microwave in short intervals of 15–30 seconds, stirring after each interval. Be careful not to overheat as chocolate can easily burn. Once the chocolate is almost melted, remove from the microwave and stir until it fully melts from the residual heat.

SEPARATING EGGS

Start with eggs at room temperature, as they are easier to separate than cold eggs. Crack the egg on a flat surface and, over a bowl, tilt the shell slightly and allow the egg white to slide out while keeping the yolk intact in the shell halves. Transfer the yolk back and forth between the shell halves, allowing the white to run into the bowl below. Be careful not to pierce the yolk. Tip the yolk into a separate bowl.

HOW TO TELL IF YOUR CAKE IS COOKED

Insert a toothpick or skewer into the centre of the cake. If it comes out clean or with just a few crumbs, the cake is done.

Alternatively, if you gently press the centre of the cake and it springs back, this is usually a sign that the cake is cooked.

GREASING AND LINING A BAKING TIN

Grease the inside of the tin using butter or non-stick cooking spray. This will help the cake easily release from the tin after baking.

Cut a piece of baking parchment to fit the bottom of the tin. Place the parchment paper in the greased tin, ensuring it lies flat and covers the entire bottom.

ROOM TEMPERATURE

Baking with room-temperature ingredients helps create a smoother batter, promotes better mixing and allows for more even leavening and baking, resulting in a more consistent and evenly baked final product. NB: Some recipes specifically call for cold butter.

HOW TO FOLD A MIXTURE CORRECTLY

1. Combine the lighter ingredients into the heavier batter using a rubber spatula.
2. Cut through the centre of the mixture and gently lift and fold the lighter ingredients into the batter.
3. Rotate the bowl as you fold to incorporate the ingredients without deflating them.
4. Repeat until the ingredients are well combined, being cautious not to over-mix.

HOW TO CREAM BUTTER AND SUGAR

1. Soften the butter to room temperature.
2. Place the softened butter and sugar in a mixing bowl.
3. Using an electric mixer or a wooden spoon, beat the butter and sugar together until light and fluffy.
4. Continue mixing until the mixture becomes pale in colour and the sugar is fully incorporated.
5. Scrape down the sides of the bowl with a spatula as needed to ensure even mixing.
6. The butter and sugar should be well creamed, creating a smooth mixture ready for further recipe steps.

QUICK COOLING

1. Remove the cake from the oven and let it cool in the tin for about 10 minutes.
2. Carefully transfer the cake from the tin to a wire rack.
3. Place the cake in the refrigerator or freezer for quicker cooling. Make sure it's not a very large cake as it may cause the fridge/freezer to rise in temperature which may spoil your food.

TEST BATCH (COOKIES)

Baking a large batch of cookies and want them to be the perfect combination of gooey and crispy? Bake a test cookie by itself first to check your timings to see if you need more or less cooking time for bigger batches.

BAKING POWDER V BICARBONATE OF SODA/BAKING SODA

Baking powder is a combination of baking soda, acid and a stabiliser, and it provides both acidity and leavening power to baked goods. Bicarb or baking soda, on the other hand, is pure sodium bicarbonate and needs an acidic ingredient to activate its leavening properties. Baking powder is used when a recipe doesn't require additional acidity, while baking soda is used when an acidic ingredient such as buttermilk is present in the recipe.

HOW TO KNOW IF YOUR BREAD IS KNEADED ENOUGH

1. Check the dough texture: properly kneaded dough should be smooth, elastic and slightly tacky.
2. Do the windowpane test: take a small piece of dough and stretch it gently between your fingers. It should stretch without tearing and form a thin, translucent piece of dough.
3. Both under-kneaded and over-kneaded dough can affect the final texture and structure of the bread. Practice will help you develop a feel for when the dough is correctly kneaded.

HOW TO TELL IF BREAD IS PROVED

1. Check for a noticeable increase in the size of the dough. It should have nearly doubled in volume.
2. Gently press a finger into the dough. If the indentation springs back slowly, the bread is properly proved. If it springs back quickly, it needs more time to rise.
3. Look for small bubbles or air pockets on the surface of the dough, indicating that the yeast has been active and fermentation has occurred.
4. A proven bread will feel airy and light rather than dense or heavy.

RUBBING BUTTER INTO FLOUR

Start by cutting cold butter into small cubes. Then rub the butter and flour together, using your fingertips until it turns to crumbs. The texture of the crumbs depends on what you're making: scones, for example, need coarse crumbs but delicate biscuits need fine breadcrumb-like crumbs. It's important to work quickly and stop once the mixture reaches the desired consistency or you could overwork it and melt the butter.

MIXING DOUGHS AND BATTER

How you mix your dough or batter will depend on the recipe. A bread dough needs to be mixed and kneaded a lot to build up that gluten structure for a well-risen, light bread. On the other hand, cake batters and biscuits require very little mixing. You want these batters or doughs mixed until JUST combined. Over-mixing risks a dense, chewy bake.

ICING A CAKE

1. Prep: ensure that your cake is fully cooled before you begin icing. It's best to level the top of the cake if it has a domed shape.
2. Layer the cake: place the first layer of cake on a serving board. Pipe a dam of icing all around the outside rim of the cake. Fill with jam, ganache or more buttercream here if you wish. Repeat until you have used up all your layers. Remember to keep the flattest layer for the top.
3. Crumb coat: apply a thin layer of icing, known as a crumb coat, all over the cake. This helps to seal in any loose crumbs and provides a smooth base for the final coat. Use an offset spatula or a palette knife to spread the icing evenly.

4. Chill the cake: place the cake in the refrigerator for 20–30 minutes to allow the crumb coat to set. This will make it easier to apply the final coat without mixing in any crumbs.

5. Final coat: take the chilled cake out and apply the final coat of icing. Start from the top and work your way down the sides, using a generous amount of icing. Use an offset spatula or palette knife to smooth the icing, holding it parallel to the cake while rotating the cake on a turntable if you have one. Continue to smooth the sides until you achieve a completely even and smooth surface.

6. Perfecting: use an offset spatula to clean up any excess icing around the edges, creating neat and straight edges. I find it handy to warm up my spatula or palette knife in a glass of warm water and then dry it, to smooth out any imperfections.

7. Decorate: once the cake is smoothly iced, you can decorate it by piping additional swirls or lettering, or adding decorations like sprinkles, fresh fruit or chocolate shavings. My favourite part!

FILLING A PIPING BAG

1. Fit a piping bag with the piping tip of your choice.
2. Place the piping bag, tip side down, into a tall glass.
3. Fold the top edges of the piping bag over the rim of the glass, creating a cuff to hold the bag in place.
4. Scoop the filling into the piping bag using a spoon or spatula.
5. Once the bag is filled, unfold the top edges and lift it out of the glass, gently pressing out any air pockets and sealing the bag at the top.
6. Twist the top of the bag to secure the filling inside and then pipe away!

CUTTING BAKES

For super-sharp cut bakes, warm a knife in a glass of hot water, wipe dry and then slice your traybakes. The perfect trick for not getting cracked chocolate, especially on millionaires' shortbread.

COLOURING YOUR BAKES/ICING

1. Choose the type of food dye: gel/paste food colouring is more concentrated and will yield vibrant colours, while liquid food colouring is more diluted and you may need more of it to achieve the desired effect. I don't advise using liquid food colouring because the extra liquid may affect your bake.

2. Start small: begin by adding a small amount of food dye to your batter or icing. It's easier to add more colour than to lighten it.

3. Mix thoroughly: mix the food dye into the batter or icing until the colour is evenly distributed. Pay attention to any lumps or streaks and continue mixing until smooth.

4. Adjust if needed: if the colour isn't as intense as you want, add a little more food dye and mix again. Repeat until you achieve your desired colour.

5. Darkening: if you're colouring icing, be aware that some colours, especially red and black, may deepen and intensify over time. It's a good idea to let the coloured icing sit for a while before using, to see if the shade changes.

FOR FLAT-TOP CAKES

1. Proper measurements: ensure accurate measurements of ingredients, as too much leavening agent (baking powder or baking soda) can cause the cake to rise unevenly and create a domed top.
2. Mixing technique: use the proper mixing technique to incorporate the ingredients evenly. Over-mixing a batter can create excess air pockets, resulting in a domed cake. Mix until just combined.
3. Proper temperature: preheat the oven to the recommended temperature. An oven thermometer will help. An oven that is too hot can cause the cake to rise unevenly.
4. Baking tin prep: grease and line your baking tins, making sure the coating is even. This will help the cake bake more evenly and release from the pans more easily.
5. Levelling the batter: after pouring the batter into the cake tins, use a spatula or the back of a spoon to level the surface. Make sure it is evenly spread to avoid any high spots.
6. Cake strips: these are little fabric strips that you soak in water and then wrap around circular cake tins. This helps the outside of the cake not to bake too fast and helps create a super-flat top on your cake for stacking. You can easily find these cake strips online.

TO CRUSH BISCUITS FOR A CHEESECAKE OR CHOCOLATE BISCUIT CAKE

1. Choose a crisp, plain biscuit: digestives work particularly well.
2. Start by breaking the biscuits into pieces. Either put them a Ziploc bag and use a rolling pin to crush them gently, or put them in a food processor and pulse until they reach the desired crumb consistency.
3. The consistency will depend on your preference and the recipe you're using. You can aim for fine crumbs for a cheesecake or various chunk sizes for a chocolate biscuit cake. Make sure to avoid pulverising them into a fine powder, as you want some texture in your bake.

COOKIES

BROWN BUTTER COOKIES

I first fell in love with browned butter in culinary school. It works amazingly well in both sweet and savoury dishes. These cookies give the perfect balance of chewy, crispy and gooey – this is a staple cookie recipe for me!

MAKES 10
PREP TIME 50 MINS
COOK TIME 10–12 MINS

125g unsalted butter
(browned)
60g light brown sugar
50g dark brown sugar
50g caster sugar
1 medium egg
1 tsp vanilla bean paste
$^1/_2$ tsp instant coffee
150g plain flour
$^1/_2$ tsp salt
$^1/_4$ tsp baking powder
$^1/_4$ tsp bicarbonate of
soda/baking soda
100g dark chocolate
bar, chopped into
rough chunks
100g milk chocolate
bar, chopped into
rough chunks
flaky salt, optional

- Place the butter in a small saucepan over a medium heat. Melt it, then let it boil until you see the milk solids sink to the bottom and turn a nice golden-brown colour. Remove from the heat and allow it to cool for 15 minutes.
- Put the browned butter and all sugars into a large mixing bowl. Whisk until combined well.
- Add in the egg and whisk until nice and fluffy. Next, mix in the vanilla and coffee powder.
- Sift in the flour, salt, baking powder and bicarbonate of soda. Fold until you have a firm dough.
- Add in the chopped-up chocolate and fold through.
- Chill the cookie dough for at least 30 minutes.
- Preheat the oven to 200°C/180°C fan/gas mark 6 and line a baking tray with baking parchment.
- Portion up 10 cookie dough balls on the baking tray. (I use an ice-cream scoop to do this.)
- Bake for 10–12 minutes.
- Remove from the oven and give the tray a light tap on a flat surface (this helps to flatten the cookies and make them level). Sprinkle on some flaky salt if you wish. Leave to cool for about 15 minutes.
- These will keep for up to three days in an airtight container.

GILL'S TIPS
Brown butter is butter you have heated up until the milk solids sink to the bottom of the pan and start to toast. This step really makes a difference, bringing the cookies to a whole new level. (It must be watched closely as it can burn easily.)

JAMMY SHORTBREAD SANDWICHES

These biscuits were my favourite growing up – they always disappeared out of the biscuit tin when I was around. A gorgeous delicate, buttery biscuit filled with a silky vanilla cream and raspberry jam.

MAKES 15
PREP TIME 1 HOUR 30 MINS
COOK TIME 15–20 MINS

Biscuit
90g salted butter
75g caster sugar
1 small egg
1 tsp vanilla extract
180g plain flour
15g cornflour

Vanilla buttercream
100g unsalted butter,
  at room temperature
200g icing sugar plus 1
  tbsp extra for serving
1 tsp vanilla extract
1–3 tsp milk

4 tbsp raspberry jam

GILL'S TIPS
If you don't have a cookie cutter, simply use a round glass.

- In a large mixing bowl, with an electric whisk, cream the butter and sugar until light and fluffy. Mix in the egg and vanilla.
- Sift in the flour and cornflour and combine until a dough comes together. Don't over-mix or it may become chewy.
- Bring your dough together into a flattened ball with your hands and wrap it in cling film or baking paper. Chill in the fridge for 20–30 minutes.
- Roll out the chilled dough on a lightly floured surface into a large rectangle about half a centimetre thick.
- Cut into any shape you like with a cookie cutter – I use a 5cm (2 inch) flower cutter, with a smaller flower cutter to cut out the centre of half of the cookies, but this is optional. Place the pieces on a baking tray and chill for a further 30 minutes.
- Preheat the oven to 190°C/170°C fan/gas mark 5. Line a baking tray with baking parchment.
- Bake the cookies for 15–20 minutes until starting to brown around the edges.
- While they're cooling, make the vanilla buttercream. Place the soft butter into a mixing bowl. Using an electric hand whisk, beat until very pale and fluffy. This will take about 5 minutes.
- Sift in the icing sugar in two separate batches and beat until incorporated well (begin at a low speed or the sugar will fly everywhere). Add the vanilla and combine. Next, add in the milk a teaspoonful at a time until you have a silky texture.
- Pipe a ring of buttercream on half the biscuits, then fill the centre with a small dollop of raspberry jam. Top with another biscuit and dust with icing sugar.
- These will keep in an airtight box for about three days.

CHOCOLATE CHIP SKILLET COOKIE

This was always my go-to dessert whenever I saw it on a restaurant menu, but not many places serve it, so of course I had to make a recipe for it! A warm cookie dough baked in a dish and served straight away with ice cream and caramel sauce on top – the tastiest dessert for two!

SERVES 2 (MAKES 1)
PREP TIME 10 MINS
COOK TIME 15–20 MINS

55g salted butter
50g light brown sugar
30g caster sugar
1 small egg
1 tsp vanilla extract
125g plain flour
1 tbsp cornflour
$\frac{1}{4}$ tsp bicarbonate of soda/baking soda
$\frac{1}{4}$ tsp baking powder
70g dark chocolate chips
70g milk chocolate chips

To serve
vanilla ice cream
caramel sauce

- Preheat the oven to 200°C/180°C fan/gas mark 6. Grease a 10–15cm (4–6 inch) baking dish or skillet.
- In a bowl, cream together the butter and both sugars with an electric whisk until light and fluffy.
- Add in the egg and vanilla, and combine.
- Sift in the flour, cornflour, bicarbonate of soda and baking powder, and mix with a spatula until you have a firm dough. Add in the chocolate chips and mix.
- Place your dough into the baking dish and flatten down. Bake for approximately 15 minutes until the top is golden.
- Serve immediately with all the toppings you wish! (I use vanilla ice cream and caramel sauce.)

GILL'S TIPS
Experiment with different flavours of ice cream and sauces and even chopped nuts.

BROOKIES

Brownie meets cookie – the ultimate combo! Cooking the brownie cookie-style gives a fudgy and soft cookie with that classic crinkly, crispy brownie top!

MAKES 10
PREP TIME 25 MINS
COOK TIME 10–12 MINS

70g unsalted butter

50g dark chocolate

1 medium egg

150g caster sugar

1 tsp espresso powder or instant coffee

50g plain flour, sieved

30g cocoa powder

$\frac{1}{4}$ tsp salt

75g chocolate chips

a few pinches of flaky salt, optional

- Melt the butter and chocolate in the microwave in a heatproof bowl in 30-second blasts, stirring regularly until fully melted. Leave to cool for a few minutes until just warm to the touch (we don't want it to cook the egg).
- Put the egg and sugar into a bowl and whisk until fluffy. Whisk in the chocolate/butter mix and coffee powder until combined.
- Sift in the flour, cocoa powder and salt, and fold. Next, fold in the chocolate chips, then leave the mixture to thicken up for about 10 minutes.
- Preheat the oven to 200°C/180°C fan/gas mark 6. Line a baking tray with baking parchment.
- Using an ice-cream scoop, scoop the mixture onto the lined baking tray – you should get about 10 cookies – and leave room between them as they will spread (you can do this in two batches or use two baking trays). Try to get them as round and even as possible. Sprinkle on top with flaky salt, if you wish.
- Bake for 10–12 minutes, then allow them to cool on the tray for about 10–15 minutes.
- These will keep for up to three days in an airtight container.

GILL'S TIPS
- It is super-important to use unsalted butter in this recipe. I have listed salt as a separate ingredient, because getting an exact measure of salt brings all the flavour profiles together to create a well-balanced brookie.
- Place some ice cream in between two brookies for an extra-special ice-cream cookie sambo!

CHOCOLATE HAZELNUT STUFFED COOKIES

Stuffing cookies is probably one of my favourite things so I had to give you a classic combo. This is a crispy and gooey cookie packed with a melting chocolate hazelnut centre, rolled in chopped hazelnuts for a crunchy, nutty coating. Once you make these, you will be HOOKED!

MAKES 10
PREP TIME 2 HOURS
COOK TIME 15–17 MINS

10 tsp chocolate hazelnut spread
110g unsalted butter
100g light brown sugar
60g caster sugar
1 large egg
1 tsp vanilla extract
250g plain flour
2 tbsp cornflour
$\frac{1}{2}$ tsp baking powder
$\frac{1}{2}$ tsp bicarbonate of soda/baking soda
$\frac{1}{2}$ tsp salt
200g milk chocolate chips
65g skinless hazelnuts, finely chopped

- Start by placing 10 teaspoonfuls of chocolate hazelnut spread on a lined tray. Pop this in the freezer for at least 30 minutes until frozen solid.
- In a large mixing bowl, cream together the butter and both sugars until light and fluffy. Add in the egg and vanilla, and whisk until smooth.
- Sift in the flour, cornflour, baking powder, bicarbonate of soda and salt. Fold until you have a firm dough. Add in the chocolate chips and mix them through.
- Weigh out the cookie dough into ten 80g portions. Mould each portion around a teaspoonful of frozen chocolate hazelnut spread.
- Roll each ball in chopped hazelnuts and place on a lined tray. Place in the freezer for at least 1 hour.
- Preheat the oven to 200°C/180°C fan/gas mark 6 for 30 minutes before baking. Bake for 15–17 minutes – do only 3 or 4 at a time as they are big! Leave to cool for about 15 minutes.
- These will keep for up to three days in an airtight container.

 GILL'S TIPS
- Chilling your cookies keeps them nice and thick with a gooey centre.
- Peanut butter fan? Swap flavours and try a peanut butter centre and roll in some chopped peanuts instead.

BUTTER SHORTBREAD

My dad's favourite biscuit has always been shortbread, so this was probably one of the first recipes I ever made growing up. One of the easiest bakes you can make, it's crisp, buttery and melt-in-the-mouth, with an added touch of luxury!

MAKES 10
PREP TIME 1 HOUR 20 MINS
COOK TIME 15–20 MINS

125g salted butter
60g caster sugar plus 1 tbsp to finish
200g plain flour

Optional extras to finish
150g chocolate (milk, dark or white – whichever you prefer), melted
2 tbsp finely chopped hazelnuts, peanuts or pistachios, orange zest, flaky salt, crushed dried raspberries, desiccated coconut or sprinkles

- Line a baking tray with baking parchment.
- In a large mixing bowl, with an electric whisk, cream the butter and sugar until light and fluffy. Add in the flour and combine until a dough comes together. If your mix is struggling to come together, add a sprinkle of water.
- Bring your dough together with your hands into a flattened ball and wrap in cling film or baking paper. Chill in the fridge for about 20–30 minutes.
- Roll out the dough into a large rectangle about 1cm (half an inch) thick on a lightly floured surface. Cut into any shape you like – I choose 10 finger-length rectangles. Place them on a baking tray, prick with a fork and then sprinkle with a small amount of caster sugar. Place in the fridge for 30 minutes.
- Preheat the oven to 190°C/170°C fan/gas mark 5.
- Bake for 15–20 minutes until the shortbread starts to brown around the edges. Cool on a wire rack.
- Serve as they are or get fancy: dip the shortbread fingers in melted chocolate and sprinkle with whatever takes your fancy: hazelnuts, peanuts, pistachios, orange zest, flaky salt, dried raspberries, desiccated coconut or sprinkles.
- These will keep for about a week in an airtight container. Enjoy!

GILL'S TIPS
- It's vital not to over-mix this dough: mix until it just comes together.
- Keeping your dough chilled will help with cutting nice shapes and will stop the shortbread from spreading in the oven.

ICE-CREAM COOKIE SAMBOS

Ice-cream cookie sambos bring me back to when I was on holidays as a kid
– they always spark joy in me!

MAKES 5
PREP TIME 1 HOUR 30 MINS
COOK TIME 15–20 MINS

125g unsalted butter
  (browned)
60g light brown sugar
50g dark brown sugar
50g caster sugar
1 medium egg
1 tsp vanilla bean paste
150g plain flour
$^1/_4$ tsp salt
$^1/_2$ tsp baking powder
$^1/_4$ tsp bicarbonate of
  soda/baking soda
100g dark chocolate
  bar, roughly chopped
100g milk chocolate
  bar, roughly chopped
flaky salt, optional
a tub of your favourite
  ice cream

- Line a baking tray with baking parchment.
- Put the butter in a small saucepan over a medium heat. Melt the butter and then let it boil until you see the milk solids sink to the bottom and turn a nice golden-brown colour. Remove from the heat and allow to cool for 15 minutes.
- In a large mixing bowl, add the browned butter and all the sugars. Whisk until combined well. Crack in the egg, add the vanilla and whisk until nice and fluffy.
- Sift in the flour, salt, baking powder and bicarbonate of soda. Fold with a spatula until you have a firm dough. Add in the chopped-up chocolate and fold through. Chill the dough in a covered bowl for at least 30 minutes.
- Preheat the oven to 200°C/180°C fan/gas mark 6.
- Portion up into 10 even cookie dough balls, approximately 65g each and place on a baking tray spaced well apart because they will spread.
- Bake for 12–14 minutes until browned around the outside. When you take them from the oven, give the tray a tap on a flat surface to release any air bubbles to ensure you get flat and even cookies. Sprinkle with some flaky salt if you wish and leave to cool completely.
- Now comes the fun part! Add as much or as little ice cream as you like on top of one cookie and then smack another cookie on top. To get the ice cream nice and round, mould it into a round cutter first. Serve immediately!

GILL'S TIPS
If you're feeling extra fancy, dip half the cookie sambos into melted chocolate!

CHOCOLATE FLORENTINES

My take on an Italian classic. A nutty almond toffee cookie dipped in and drizzled with chocolate.

MAKES 10
PREP TIME 2 HOURS 25
   MINS
COOK TIME: 12–14 MINS

100g flaked almonds
50g unsalted butter
100g golden syrup
50g light brown sugar
pinch of salt
150g chocolate (dark
   or milk)

GILL'S TIPS
• Swap out the 100g almonds for different nuts or dried fruit combos, making sure to keep to the same quantity (e.g. 50g almonds, 25g pistachios and 25g walnuts).
• I use a round cookie cutter to shape the mix. This gives a nice round cookie.

• Preheat the oven to 200°C/180°C fan/gas mark 6. Line a baking tray with baking parchment. Toast your almonds in the oven for about 10 minutes until lightly golden.

• Put the butter, golden syrup and sugar in a large saucepan over a medium heat. Bring to the boil and simmer for about 5 minutes while constantly stirring. Once it has thickened to a honey-like consistency, remove from the heat and then mix in the toasted almonds and a pinch of salt.

• Spoon the mixture into 10 evenly sized dollops onto the lined baking tray and then flatten down into a round cookie shape. If you want to get them very round, put the mix into a round cutter and squish down with a spoon. Chill in the fridge until set – this will take about an hour.

• When the cookies have set, melt the chocolate in a heatproof bowl in the microwave until smooth. Stir every 30 seconds to prevent it burning.

• Dip the base of the cookies into the melted chocolate and then place back onto the tray, chocolate side down. Drizzle the remaining chocolate over your cookies. Place the tray back into the fridge until the chocolate hardens – this will take about an hour.

• These will keep for up to three days in an airtight container.

SNACKS

FLUFFY AMERICAN PANCAKES

These fluffy, light pancakes are perfect for your favourite pancake toppings – rashers and maple syrup, the traditional Irish lemon juice and sugar, Biscoff, Nutella, jam, fresh strawberries, chopped bananas, blueberries, or whatever you fancy yourself!

MAKES 4–12 PANCAKES
PREP TIME 15 MINS
COOK TIME 15–20 MINS

220g plain flour
250ml buttermilk
50g salted butter,
  melted
40g caster sugar
2 tsp baking powder
1 tsp vanilla extract
2 eggs

- Get all your toppings of choice ready to go.
- Put a large frying pan onto a medium heat to warm up while you make the batter.
- Put all the ingredients into a large bowl and whisk till smooth.
- Lightly grease the pan and keep on a medium heat.
- Ladle a small amount of batter onto the pan, and do only one or two pancakes at a time. (Don't worry if your first pancake is a flop: this almost always happens!)
- After about 2 minutes, once bubbles begin to form on top of the pancake, carefully flip it over and cook for another 2 minutes until light and golden.
- Repeat until all the pancakes are cooked.
- Now comes the fun part – creating some delicious stacks of pancakes with all your tasty toppings! Eat immediately.

GILL'S TIPS
Use an ice-cream scoop when placing your batter into the pan to get evenly sized pancakes.

PEANUT MILK CHOCOLATE OAT BARS

A delicious, soft flapjack oat bar packed with crunchy peanuts and milk chocolate chips, this perfect midweek snack is super versatile – you can play around with many different flavour combinations.

MAKES 8
PREP TIME 1 HOUR 15 MINS
COOK TIME 20–25 MINS

175g salted butter

190g light brown sugar

115g golden syrup

1 tsp vanilla extract

420g oats

100g milk chocolate chips

100g unsalted peanuts, roughly chopped

- Preheat the oven to 200°C/180°C fan/gas mark 6. Grease a 20 x 20cm (8 x 8 inch) square tin with spray oil or butter and then line with baking parchment.
- Place the butter, sugar, golden syrup and vanilla in a medium saucepan over a gentle heat. Mix continually until it is just melted (about 5 minutes). Set aside for approximately 5 minutes to cool.
- Pour the mix over the oats and stir until fully incorporated.
- Fold in the chocolate chips and peanuts and then tip the mix into the baking tray. Flatten down until smooth.
- Bake for approximately 20 minutes until just the edges begin to brown.
- Allow your bake cool completely on a wire rack. When cool, put the tray in the fridge to chill for about an hour (this helps with cutting).
- Cut your bake into fingers. (I usually cut mine into 8 bars.) Drizzle with some extra melted chocolate if you wish.
- These will keep for five days in an airtight container.

GILL'S TIPS
Swap out the 100g peanuts for hazelnuts or any other nut to change up the flavour.

TOASTER POP PASTRIES

This fun bake is a childhood favourite of mine – but better! Buttery, flaky pastry stuffed with sweet jam and topped with that classic icing and sprinkles!

MAKES 4
PREP TIME 1 HOUR 30 MINS
COOK TIME 20–25 MINS

150g plain flour
30g caster sugar
100g salted butter,
   cubed
50ml water
4 tbsp jam
1 egg, beaten, for egg
   wash

extras
4 tbsp icing sugar
sprinkles

GILL'S TIPS
Use any flavour jam or sweet spread to fill your pop pastries. Save time and use shop-bought shortcrust or puff pastry, whichever you prefer.

- Line a large flat baking tray with baking parchment.
- Place the flour and sugar in a large bowl and give it a quick stir. Rub in the cubed butter between your fingertips until the mixture resembles breadcrumbs. Next, add the water, one tablespoonful at a time, and mix until a dough forms.
- Bring the dough together into a ball, then wrap in baking parchment and chill in the fridge for 30 minutes.
- Preheat the oven to 200°C/180°C fan/gas mark 6.
- When the dough is chilled, roll it out onto a lightly floured surface into a rectangle approximately 25 x 32cm (10 x 12 inches). Cut this rectangle into 8 smaller rectangles.
- Fill the centre of 4 rectangles with a tablespoonful of jam each (it will spread when baking). Damp the margin with egg wash, then cover with the other 4 rectangles and seal all the sides of each pop pastry with a fork. Finally, pierce each top twice to allow steam to escape.
- Place your pop pastries on the baking tray and chill for a further 30 minutes. Once chilled, brush them with egg wash and bake for 20–25 minutes until golden.
- Allow to cool on a wire rack. Once cooled, mix the icing sugar with a teaspoonful of water at a time until you have a very thick, honey-like texture.
- Using a spoon or a piping bag, create a square of icing on top of the pop pastries. Top with sprinkles and tuck in!
- The pop pastries will keep for two days in an airtight container.

BUTTERMILK SCONES

A classic scone, fluffy, buttery and with a crisp edge. Using buttermilk to make scones was a game changer for me and I havent looked back. It gives incredible flavour and texture. Top with cream and jam for an unbeatable treat!

MAKES 6
PREP TIME 15 MINS
COOK TIME 20–25 MINS

220ml buttermilk
1 tsp vanilla extract
1 egg
500g self-raising flour
$1/_2$ tsp baking powder
50g caster sugar
115g salted butter, cold and cubed

Optional
1 egg, beaten, for egg wash

- Preheat the oven to 200°C/180°C fan/gas mark 6. Line a baking tray with parchment.
- In a small bowl, whisk together the buttermilk, vanilla and egg. Set aside.
- Sift the flour and baking powder into a large bowl and add the sugar and cubed butter. Rub the butter into the flour until you have a coarse texture (not breadcrumbs, as that would be too fine).
- Make a well in the centre of the large bowl and then pour in the wet mix. Gently bring together with a spatula.
- Fold the dough very gently to form a smooth ball. On a floured surface, using a rolling pin or your hands, flatten it to a thickness of 3–4cm (1½ inches).
- Using a round cutter or a glass, make 6 even scones with your dough. Flour the cutter before every stamp so that it doesn't stick. The less you work with this dough the better.
- Put the scones onto the baking tray and brush with an egg wash on top (optional).
- Bake for 20–25 minutes or until the base has a nice colour.
- Leave to cool before serving with jam and cream or butter.
- These will keep for two days in an airtight container.

 GILL'S TIPS

- If you dont have buttermilk, you can use the equivalent amount of full fat milk with a tablespoonful of lemon juice mixed through it. Do this about 5 minutes before baking to let the lemon juice work into the milk.
- For a fruity scone, add a handful of raisins, raspberries, blueberries or chopped-up pear to your scone mix.

PEANUT BUTTER PROTEIN BITES

Shop-bought protein bars can be pricey. I love making my own version. A big batch takes only a few minutes to prep, ready to snack on when needed.

MAKES 10
PREP TIME 35 MINS

50g oats
30g protein powder
70g peanut butter
  (smooth or crunchy)
50g honey
pinch of cinnamon
handful of chocolate
  chips (optional)

- Line a baking tray with baking parchment.
- Place all the ingredients in a bowl. Mix until well combined.
- Roll your mix into 10 even balls, about 20g each, and place on the parchment.
- Cool in the fridge to set for about 30 minutes and then store in an airtight container at room temperature.
- These will keep for up to a week.

 GILL'S TIPS
Drizzle with melted chocolate for an extra treat!

CHOCOLATE CAKE-IN-A-MUG

Want a quick cake fix? This is the one for you! Rich, chocolatey and FAST. This recipe was created one night when I had nothing sweet in the house and oh boy!

SERVES 1
PREP TIME 5 MINS
COOK TIME 2–3 MINS

10g salted butter
25g dark chocolate
1 small egg
45g light brown sugar
35g self-raising flour
5g cocoa powder
2 tbsp milk
20g chocolate chips

Optional extras
1 scoop of ice cream
a drizzle of caramel or
  chocolate sauce (or
  both!)

- Put in the butter and dark chocolate in a large mug. Melt in the microwave for about 30 seconds until just melted, then leave to cool for a few minutes.
- Add in the rest of the ingredients and mix until smooth with a small spatula or spoon.
- Place your mug back into the microwave for 1½–2 minutes or until a toothpick comes out clean.
- Tuck in while it's still warm!

GILL'S TIPS
Top with some ice cream to take it to another level. Caramel or chocolate sauce would also be super tasty!

CHOCOLATE STUFFED FRENCH TOAST

This is my favourite Sunday brunch treat! Sweet buttery brioche stuffed with chocolate hazelnut spread, fried and then dipped in cinnamon sugar. Sweet brunch HEAVEN!

SERVES 4
PREP TIME 20 MINS
COOK TIME 15–20 MINS

$^1/_4$ tsp cinnamon

100g caster sugar

3 eggs

1 tsp vanilla extract

50ml milk

8 slices brioche bread
(approx. 1 cm/$^1/_2$ inch
thick)

4 tbsp chocolate
hazelnut spread

any additional toppings
you fancy, such as
a handful of fresh
berries or chopped
nuts, or a drizzle of
maple syrup

- Place a frying pan on a medium heat.
- In a bowl, mix the cinnamon and sugar. Set aside.
- In a large bowl, mix the eggs, vanilla and milk.
- Grab 8 slices of brioche. Put a tablespoonful of chocolate spread into the centre of 4 slices. Top each of these with another slice of brioche and pinch the edges to seal them slightly.
- Quickly dip each sandwich into the egg mixture, to coat the outside, and then fry for 2–3 minutes each side until golden brown.
- While still warm, dip a slice at a time into the bowl of cinnamon sugar, and coat evenly.
- Serve with any toppings you like. Eat straight away while you have a lovely melty centre.

GILL'S TIPS
Fill your French toast with any other spread you like, e.g. peanut butter, jam, Biscoff spread or caramel sauce.

HOMEMADE GRANOLA

A staple recipe that couldn't be easier to put together! Keep it in a jar for delicious granola whenever you need it – much better than any shop-bought granola. My favourite part of this recipe is changing it up every time I make it with whatever I have in the cupboards: peanuts, hazelnuts, walnuts, raisins, dried orange peel, dried mango, maybe even some desiccated coconut! You really can't go wrong with your flavour combinations!

SERVES 6
PREP TIME 15 MINS
COOK TIME 20–25 MINS

30g coconut oil, melted
100g oats
100g nuts/seeds
$^1/_4$ tsp cinnamon
1 tsp vanilla extract
75g honey
50g dried fruit

- Preheat the oven to 180°C/160°C fan/gas mark 4. Line a baking tray with baking parchment.
- In a heatproof bowl, melt the coconut oil (this takes just a few seconds).
- Place the rest of the ingredients except for the dried fruit in a large bowl and add the coconut oil. Mix well until everything is coated in the wet ingredients.
- Spread the mix onto the baking tray and bake for 20–25 minutes.
- Once baked, mix in the dried fruit and leave to cool.
- Store your granola in a jar (it will keep for up to two weeks).
- Serve however you like!

GILL'S TIPS
Add some chocolate chips, once cooled, for an extra treat!

BREADS

FLATBREAD PIZZAS

This is one of my go-to recipes. I make this simple flatbread on repeat.
The easiest pizza you'll ever make!

MAKES 2
PREP TIME 40 MINS
COOK TIME 20 MINS

250g self-raising flour
pinch of salt
I tsp baking powder
250ml Greek yogurt
I tsp olive oil
150g shop-bought
  pizza sauce
100g mozzarella,
  grated
your favourite pizza
  toppings: any
  combination of sliced
  pepperoni, sausage,
  cooked ham, roasted
  chicken, jalapenos,
  basil, roasted veg,
  sweetcorn, onions,
  honey, rocket, chilli
  flakes, mushrooms

- Preheat the oven to 200°C/180°C fan/gas mark 6. Line two baking trays with baking parchment.
- Place the flour, salt and baking powder in a large bowl and give it a quick stir. Add the yoghurt and oil. Mix until everything is incorporated.
- Place a cloth over the bowl and let it rest for 20 minutes at room temperature.
- Once it has rested, split the dough in two. Roll each piece out into a pizza shape and place them on the baking trays.
- Bake in the oven for 5–10 minutes until starting to brown around the edges.
- Remove them from the oven and spread with pizza sauce, and sprinkle on the mozzarella and any toppings you like. Return to the oven to cook for about 10 minutes until melty and golden.
- Tuck in!

 GILL'S TIPS
Turn these into cheesy garlic bread by using garlic butter instead of the pizza sauce and sprinkling cheese on top. Alternatively, keep them plain, fry them in a pan and serve with a curry.

IRISH STOUT BROWN BREAD

A super-quick and easy stout bread that tastes absolutely amazing smothered in butter! It takes a few minutes to put together and stays fresh for days (if it lasts that long!)

MAKES 1 LOAF (12
  GENEROUS SLICES)
PREP TIME 10 MINS
COOK TIME 40–45 MINS

350g wholemeal flour
100g plain flour
50g oats
1 tsp light brown sugar
1 tsp salt
**2 tsp bicarbonate of
  soda/baking soda**
**50g salted butter,
  cubed**
200ml buttermilk
200ml Irish stout
2 tbsp treacle

Optional
**30g mixed seeds (e.g.
  pumpkin, sesame,
  poppy and/or hemp
  seeds)**

- Preheat the oven to 200°C/180°C fan/gas mark 6. Grease a 900g (2 lb) loaf tin with spray oil or butter and then line it with baking parchment (greasing the tin helps the parchment to cling to the sides nicely).
- In a large bowl, place both flours, oats, sugar, salt and bicarbonate of soda, and mix. Add in some seeds here if you like. Add the cubed butter and rub it into the flour until you have the texture of breadcrumbs.
- In a separate bowl, mix your buttermilk, stout and treacle. Pour this mixture into the dry ingredients. Stir until everything is just combined and you have a nice thick batter. Spoon it into the loaf tin.
- Top with some extra seeds and oats if you like and then bake for 40–45 minutes until a skewer comes out clean or the centre reaches 75°C+ on a thermometer.
- Allow to cool for about 15 minutes in the tin before removing onto a wire rack and letting it cool completely.
- Store in an airtight container for up to three days (or freeze in slices).

 GILL'S TIPS
I use a wholemeal flour with seeds in it for extra flavour but feel free to add some extra seeds into the dough.

BRIOCHE BURGER BUNS

Brioche bread seems daunting as it can be quite sticky to work with (use a stand mixer if possible: mixing by hand can get very messy and tiring) but don't be intimidated. Once your dough proves it becomes a lot easier to work with. Perfect for homemade burgers!

MAKES 8
PREP TIME 2 HOURS
COOK TIME 15–18 MINS

400g plain flour
5g salt
7g instant dry yeast (I sachet)
45g sugar
75g unsalted butter
225ml milk
4 eggs plus I for egg wash
I tbsp sesame seeds

GILL'S TIPS
Top with poppy seeds for a different flavour.

- Sift the flour and salt into a stand mixer or a mixing bowl. Add the yeast, sugar and butter and rub in until you have the texture of breadcrumbs. Add in the milk and eggs and knead until dough comes away from the side of the bowl and is slightly springy. This will take about 10 minutes in a stand mixer or 15–20 minutes if kneading by hand. The dough will be sticky but that's okay.
- Place the dough in an oiled bowl and cover with cling film or a damp tea towel. Allow it to prove until doubled in size. This will take about an hour in a warm spot in the kitchen or in the airing cupboard.
- Line a baking tray with baking parchment.
- When the dough has risen, place it on a generously floured surface. Divide it into 8 equal pieces (about 100g each.) Shape into even, round balls. Place each ball onto the lined tray (use two trays if needed, to allow space for them to rise). Cover with a tea towel. Prove until the balls have puffed up and the dough slowly springs back when you press it (about 30 minutes).
- Preheat the oven to 200°C/180°C fan/gas mark 6 half an hour before baking.
- Before baking, crack the extra egg into a bowl and whisk. Brush each roll with the egg wash, then sprinkle with sesame seeds.
- Bake for 15–18 minutes until golden brown.
- Leave the buns to cool on a wire rack, then make up some delicious burgers or sandwiches and enjoy!
- They will keep for a day in an airtight container or can be wrapped individually and frozen for up to a month.

CINNAMON ROLLS

Soft, fluffy sweet dough swirled with a buttery cinnamon filling, topped with a silky cream cheese frosting and a touch of orange zest. A cosy, warm bake at its finest!

MAKES 12
PREP TIME 2 HOURS 30 MINS
COOK TIME 20–25 MINS

Dough
200ml milk
7g instant dry yeast (1 sachet)
100g caster sugar
520g plain flour
6g salt
2 eggs
50g unsalted butter, cold and cubed
1 egg, beaten, for egg wash

Cinnamon sugar
150g salted butter
150g light brown sugar
15g cinnamon

Icing
150g cream cheese
1 tsp vanilla extract
65g icing sugar
30ml double cream

zest of an orange

- Heat the milk in the microwave until slightly warm to touch (not too hot or it will kill the yeast). Put the warm milk, yeast and sugar in a mixing bowl/stand mixer and mix gently, then leave for 2 minutes.
- Next, sift in the flour and salt, add the eggs and set the mixer on a medium speed. (If mixing by hand, use a spatula until everything comes together and then use your hands.)
- Once combined, add in the cubes of butter one at a time. Knead for about 8–10 minutes until dough comes together to form a smooth ball. (If you are doing it by hand, it will take 15–20 minutes.) The dough will be a little sticky to start with but that's okay: it will come together and become smooth when kneaded.
- Once formed into a ball, place the dough in an oiled bowl. Cover with a damp towel or cling film. Let it prove at room temperature until it has doubled in size. This can take 1–2 hours and will vary depending on the temperature of the room.
- While the dough is rising, make the sugar filling. Simply whisk the butter, sugar and cinnamon in a bowl until creamy, then place to one side.
- Grease a large baking tray and line with baking parchment.
- Once the dough has doubled in size, tip it out onto a floured surface. Roll it out into a rectangle about 45 x 35cm (18 x 14 inches). Evenly spread the cinnamon sugar over it.
- Now roll up the dough, from one long side to the other, making sure it's very tight so you get a nice swirled pattern.
- Slice the rolled-up dough into 12 even portions.

- Place the cinnamon rolls on the tray, allowing space for them to rise. Cover with cling film or a damp towel and sit in a warm spot until the rolls are puffed up and jiggly. This will take about 30 minutes.
- About 15 minutes before this second proving is done, preheat the oven to 200°C/180°C fan/gas mark 6.
- Remove the towel/cling film, brush the cinnamon rolls with an egg wash and place in the oven. Bake for 20–25 minutes until golden brown.
- While the rolls are baking, make the icing: mix together your cream cheese, vanilla, icing sugar and double cream until thick and spreadable.
- When the rolls have mostly cooled, spread the icing over them and finish with a sprinkle of orange zest.
- These are best eaten on the day of making but they'll keep overnight in an airtight container in the fridge.

 GILL'S TIPS

Warm up your cinnamon rolls in the microwave the next day to refresh them!

PESTO AND CHEDDAR TWISTS

This is a go-to party treat that everyone loves! Go sweet or savoury and fill them with any type of cheese or spread, sliced veggies or fruits.

MAKES 8
PREP TIME 1 HOUR 45 MINS
COOK TIME 20–30 MINS

450g plain flour
1½ tsp salt
1 tsp caster sugar
7g instant dry yeast (1 sachet)
300ml warm water
1 tbsp olive oil
150g pesto
100g cheese, grated (use your favourite – mine is cheddar)
1 egg, beaten, for egg wash

Garlic butter
30g salted butter
1–2 cloves garlic, peeled and minced

- Sift the flour and salt into a stand mixer or a mixing bowl, add the sugar and yeast and give it a quick stir. Add the water and oil and, using your hands or a dough hook, mix together. Knead for about 8–10 minutes until the dough comes together to form a smooth ball. (If you are doing it by hand it will take 15–20 minutes.) The dough will be a little sticky to start with but that's okay: it will be nice and smooth once ready.
- Place the dough in a lightly oiled bowl and cover with cling film or a damp towel. Allow it to prove until doubled in size. It usually takes 1 hour in a warm spot.
- Line a baking tray with baking parchment.
- Once the dough has doubled in size, tip it out onto a floured surface. Roll out into a rectangle 45 x 40cm (18 x 15 inches).
- Spread the pesto on half of the rectangle and then top with the grated cheese.
- Fold the other side of the dough on top of the filled side, and pinch the edges to seal them. Cut into 8 long strips. Twist each strip a couple of times and then place on your baking tray. Leave to prove for about 20–30 minutes until lightly puffed up. Halfway through proving, pre-heat the oven to 200°C/180°C fan/gas mark 6.
- Brush the twists with an egg wash and then bake for 20–30 minutes until golden.
- While your twists are baking, make the garlic butter. In a heatproof bowl, melt the butter in short blasts in the microwave, then stir in the minced garlic.
- When you remove the twists from the oven, brush them with the garlic butter and serve hot!

CRUSTY WHITE LOAF

Is there anything better than a crusty warm loaf of bread? If you are looking to make a simple but delicious loaf of bread, this is the recipe for you.

MAKES 1 MEDIUM-SIZED
LOAF (12 GENEROUS
SLICES)
PREP TIME 2 HOURS 30 MINS
COOK TIME 50 MINS

280ml warm water

7g instant dry yeast (1 sachet)

1 tsp sugar

450g plain flour

1½ tsp salt

GILL'S TIPS
A hot baking dish gives your bread optimum opportunity for a crispy crust!

- Place the warm water, yeast and sugar in your stand mixer bowl with a dough hook and leave for 5 minutes.
- Sift in the flour and salt and knead for 10–15 minutes until the dough comes away from the sides of the bowl.
- Place the dough in a lightly oiled bowl, cover with cling film or a damp tea towel and leave to prove until doubled in size. This will take 1–1½ hours, depending on the temperature of your kitchen.
- When the dough has doubled in size, tip it onto a floured surface. Gently mould it into a round loaf and place it in a bowl lined with a cloth that has been sprinkled with flour (or in a floured proving basket, if you have one). Cover with a cloth and leave to prove until doubled in size (this will take about an hour).
- Preheat the oven to 240°C/220°C fan/gas mark 9. Put a lidded pot in the oven to preheat.
- When the dough is proved, cut a round of parchment paper slightly larger than your bowl, place it on top of the bowl and flip it over onto a flat surface.
- Carefully lift the parchment with the dough on top into the heated pot. Mind your fingers! Score the top of your dough with four stripes or a couple of diagonal slits if you prefer.
- Cover with the heated lid and bake for 30 minutes. Then remove the lid and bake for another 20 minutes. If you want a darker colour on the base, remove the bread from the pot and place on the oven rack for the last 5 minutes. The bread is cooked when you tap on the base and it sounds hollow.
- Allow to cool completely on a wire rack before slicing it up.
- This will keep for 1–2 days in an airtight container or can be frozen.

OVERNIGHT FOCACCIA

Such LITTLE effort to make an incredibly tasty piece of bread. I love making this and trying loads of different ingredients as toppings. Perfect for dinner parties!

SERVES 10
PREP TIME 1½ HOURS
　　PLUS 12–24 HOURS FOR
　　PROVING
COOK TIME 30 MINS

500g plain flour

10g salt

1 tsp caster sugar

7g instant dry yeast (1 sachet)

2 tsp olive oil and extra to drizzle

450ml water

Toppings

100g pitted olives, halved

75g sundried tomatoes

1 tbsp chopped fresh rosemary

- Sift the flour and salt into a large bowl, add the sugar, yeast, olive oil and water and mix until just combined.
- Cover with a cloth. Allow to sit for 20 minutes, then fold the dough from the sides into the centre with wet hands. Cover again and allow to sit for another 20 minutes. Repeat the last step twice more so that you have done 3 folds in total.
- Grease a baking dish with plenty of olive oil and place a sheet of baking parchment at the bottom. Put in the dough and spread it out with your fingers. Cover in cling film and place in the fridge for 12–24 hours.
- Remove the dough from the fridge 2 hours before baking.
- Preheat the oven to 220°C/200°C fan/gas mark 7.
- Using your fingers as though you're typing, spread out the dough to get the iconic dimpled look. (Oil your fingers so they don't get stuck.) Top the dough with whatever you fancy – my favourite combo is olives, sundried tomato and rosemary – and of course an extra drizzle of olive oil.
- Bake for approximately 30 minutes until golden brown.
- Brush with some olive oil and tuck in.
- This will keep for two days in an airtight container.

GILL'S TIPS
Other ideas for toppings include:

- half a courgette, thinly sliced
- 2 tbsp sliced roasted garlic
- 1 tsp fresh thyme
- 50g grated parmesan
- 75g pepper, thinly sliced
- 1 red onion, thinly sliced.

CHEESY GARLIC PULL-APART BREAD

✳ ✳ ✳

Soft white bread rolls coated in a herby garlic butter and layered with melty cheese. This is a quick and fun bread recipe that tastes unbelievably good! A perfect starter or side dish for any meal.

SERVES 4
PREP TIME 1 HOUR 45 MINS
COOK TIME 30–35 MINS

450g plain flour

1¹/₂ tsp salt

1 tsp caster sugar

7g instant dry yeast (1 sachet)

300ml warm water

150g salted butter

3 cloves garlic, minced

handful fresh parsley, chopped

100g mozzarella, grated

- Sift the flour and salt into a stand mixer or a mixing bowl and add the sugar and yeast. Add the water and mix together.
- Knead for 8–10 minutes until dough comes together to form a smooth ball. (If you are doing it by hand, it will take 15–20 minutes.) This dough will be a little sticky to start with but that's okay – it will come together and be smooth when kneaded.
- Place in a lightly oiled bowl and cover with cling film or a damp towel. Let it prove till doubled in size. This takes about an hour in a warm spot in the kitchen or the airing cupboard.
- While your dough is proving, make the garlic butter. Mince the garlic to a paste and chop up the parsley very finely. In a heatproof bowl, melt the butter in the microwave for about 30 seconds. Mix the garlic and parsley into the butter, then set aside.
- Line a 900g (2lb) loaf tin with baking parchment.
- Once the dough has doubled in size, remove it onto a floured surface. Portion up the dough into about 30 small balls. The smaller the balls, the more pull-apart pieces you have; the bigger the balls, the fewer. Do what you like here as it will bake in the same time.
- To assemble the bread, dip each dough ball into the melted garlic butter and layer the balls in the loaf tin. When you have one layer covering the base of the tin, scatter on a handful of grated mozzarella. Repeat until you have used up all the dough balls. Once assembled, sprinkle a small amount of grated cheese on top.

- Cover with cling film or a damp towel and allow to prove again for 20–30 minutes.
- Preheat the oven to 200°C/180°C fan/gas mark 6.
- Bake the bread for 30–35 minutes until golden brown. Allow it to rest for 5–10 minutes in the tin, then remove and brush some extra garlic butter on top. Serve with the leftover butter in a small dish for dipping.
- Best eaten straight away but it will keep in an airtight container for a day.

GILL'S TIPS

Want to know if your dough has risen enough? Press your finger gently into it. If it springs back straight away, it needs more time. If you press it and the indentation springs back very slowly, you are ready to go! If it doesn't spring back at all, you may have let it prove too long.

SAVOURY BAKES

HASH BROWN BREAKFAST MUFFINS

A perfect quick breakfast dish? I think so! With crisp potato edges, salty bacon and a soft egg centre, this fun breakfast bake will become a firm favourite.

MAKES 8
PREP TIME 20 MINS
COOK TIME 30–35 MINS

8 large frozen hash browns (approx. 85g each)
butter, for greasing
50g bacon lardons
50g grated cheese
8 eggs
salt and pepper
½ tsp smoked paprika
1 tbsp torn fresh parsley

- Thaw 8 hash browns. Each should fit in a cup in a muffin tray, but if your hash browns are small, use 2 per cup.
- Preheat the oven to 200°C/180°C fan/gas mark 6.
- Grease a cupcake tray with butter. Press the thawed hash browns into the cupcake tray, making sure they are nice and tight all around the sides and bottom.
- Place into the oven and bake for about 20 minutes until golden.
- While the hash browns are cooking, put a small frying pan over a medium heat with a splash of oil and fry the lardons for a couple of minutes until lightly browned.
- When the hash browns are baked, remove the tray from the oven and fill the cups with the bacon lardons. Divide the grated cheese between the cups, and then crack an egg into each cup. Season with salt and pepper and sprinkle a little smoked paprika on top.
- Return the tray to the oven to cook the egg. This will take 10–15 minutes. (You'll know the egg is cooked if the white no longer jiggles when you shake the tray.)
- Garnish with parsley and serve immediately.

 GILL'S TIPS
Swap the full egg for an omelette-like filling: crack the eggs into a bowl and beat, then add in your cooked bacon, cheese and seasonings. Mix, then divide among the cups and cook as above.

'NDUJA JAMBONS

I am obsessed with hot and spicy 'nduja (pronounced 'en-DOO-yah') sausage. Despite the French-sounding name, these ham and cheese pastries have been an Irish deli classic for decades.

SERVES 6
PREP TIME 40 MINS
COOK TIME 20–25 MINS

20g salted butter
15g plain flour
200ml milk
120g cheddar cheese, grated
salt and pepper
1 roll puff pastry
6 tbsp cooked 'nduja, crumbled
1 egg, beaten, for egg wash

Optional
2 handfuls grated cheese to top

- For the cheese sauce, place the butter in a medium saucepan over a medium heat. When it's melted, add the flour and stir for 1–2 minutes to let it cook. Add the milk a little at a time, whisking continually until you have a sauce that's thick and smooth. Stir in your cheese and mix until smooth. Season with salt and pepper. Leave aside to cool.
- Remove the puff pastry from the fridge 10–15 minutes before using. Preheat the oven to 200°C/180°C fan/gas mark 6. Line a baking tray with baking parchment.
- Unroll the sheet of puff pastry. Cut it into 6 even squares and place them on the lined baking tray. Spoon the cheese sauce onto the centre of each square. Make sure to use up all the sauce.
- Sprinkle over the 'nduja and then fold the corners of the pastry squares into the centre to create your jambon shape. Carefully brush the pastry with some beaten egg. Sprinkle some extra cheese on top (this is optional) and bake for 20–25 minutes until nice and golden.
- Leave to cool for a few minutes then tuck in!

 GILL'S TIPS
Here are some other ideas for jambon fillings:

- ham and cheese
- pepperoni and mozzarella
- roasted red pepper and goat's cheese
- pesto and Parmesan
- red onion and blue cheese
- fajita-seasoned chicken and cheddar

CHEDDAR AND CHIVE SCONES

A staple savoury bake perfect for any occasion. A soft buttermilk scone packed full of cheddar cheese and chive flavour. Serve warm with plenty of salted butter for an incredible savoury snack.

MAKES 8
PREP TIME 30 MINS
COOK TIME 20–25 MINS

225ml buttermilk
I egg
500g self-raising flour
$^1/_2$ tsp baking powder
150g grated cheddar
  (plus a little extra for
  topping, optional)
115g salted butter, cold
  and cubed
15g chopped chives
I tsp caster sugar
I egg, beaten, for egg
  wash
butter, to serve

GILL'S TIPS
Play around with different types of cheese or herbs. Here are some ideas:

• Parmesan and basil
• blue cheese and chervil
• feta and oregano
• Swiss cheese and dill

• Preheat the oven to 200°C/180°C fan/gas mark 6. Line a baking tray with baking parchment.
• In a small bowl, whisk together the buttermilk and egg. Set aside.
• Sift the flour and baking powder into a large bowl and add the grated cheese, cubed butter, chives and sugar. Rub the butter into the flour to a coarse texture (you don't want it as fine as breadcrumbs).
• Make a well in the centre and pour in the wet mix. Gently bring the mixture together.
• Carefully fold the dough together to form a smooth ball and tip it onto a floured surface. Using a rolling pin or your hands, flatten it down. This recipe makes 8 large scones that are nice and thick. So, using a round cutter, make 8 even scones with your dough. Flour the cutter on every stamp so that it doesn't stick. The less you work with this dough the better, to keep the scones light and fluffy.
• Place the scones onto the baking tray and brush the egg wash on top. Sprinkle on some extra grated cheese (if you wish).
• Bake for 20–25 minutes or until the base has a nice colour and the scones sound hollow when you tap the base.
• Allow the scones to cool a little on a wire rack, then serve while they're still warm. For extra deliciousness, cut in half and butter generously.
• Best eaten on the day of making but can be revived in the microwave the next day.

PIZZA ROLLS

Love pizza? Love pastry? This is for you: pizza-flavoured pastry rolls! Sweet tomato sauce,
pepperoni and gooey mozzarella cheese – savoury heaven!
Serve with extra tomato sauce for dipping.

MAKES 12
PREP TIME 15 MINS
COOK TIME 20 MINS

1 roll puff pastry
150g tomato sauce
100g pepperoni, sliced
125g mozzarella,
   grated
handful of fresh basil,
   torn, plus a pinch for
   garnish
1 egg, beaten, for egg
   wash

- Take the puff pastry out of the fridge 10–15 minutes before
  using, to prevent it cracking.
- Preheat the oven to 200°C/180°C fan/gas mark 6. Line a
  baking tray with baking parchment.
- Unroll the sheet of puff pastry. Spread the tomato sauce all
  over your pastry and top with the slices of pepperoni. Sprinkle
  on the grated mozzarella and some torn-up basil leaves.
- Next, roll up the pastry from one long side to the other.
  Make sure to roll it up as tightly as possible, then slice the roll
  into 12 even slices and place on the baking tray.
- Brush each roll with an egg wash and bake for approximately
  20 minutes until golden brown.
- Serve immediately or leave to cool on a wire rack. These can
  be eaten cold or warmed back up in the oven.

 GILL'S TIPS

Play around with the flavours in this recipe. Any sauce, cheese, meat
or veg will work perfectly, for example:

Meats	Veggies	Sauces
Shredded cooked chicken	sliced roast pepper	red pesto
Sliced cooked turkey	sliced onion	green pesto
Sliced salami		olive tapenade
Sliced prosciutto		red onion jam

PUFF PASTRY TARTLETS

A quick and easy savoury bake that can be tweaked and tailored to your taste! These just scream holidays in the sun for me, a lovely light and fresh taste. A variety of good-quality fresh tomatoes is essential for flavour and look!

MAKES 8
PREP TIME 30 MINS
COOK TIME 20–25 MINS

1 roll of puff pastry
200g mascarpone
    cheese
50g Parmesan cheese
2 cloves garlic, crushed
$1/4$ tsp dried oregano
$1/4$ tsp chilli flakes
pinch of fresh thyme
salt and pepper
200g (approx.) fresh
    tomatoes, sliced
1 egg, beaten, for egg
    wash
2 tbsp basil pesto

Optional
handful fresh basil, to
    garnish

- Remove the puff pastry from the fridge 10–15 minutes before using. Preheat the oven to 200°C/180°C fan/gas mark 6. Line a baking tray with baking parchment.
- Unroll the sheet of puff pastry, cut it into 8 even rectangles and place them on the baking tray.
- Put the mascarpone, Parmesan, crushed garlic, oregano, chilli, thyme, salt and pepper in a large bowl. Mix until well combined and then spread in the centre of each piece of pastry, leaving a small rim around all the edges. Top with slices of tomato.
- Brush the edges of each pastry with an egg wash.
- Bake for 20–25 minutes until golden, then dot with basil pesto and garnish with fresh basil (optional).
- Best served immediately, but can be eaten cold.

GILL'S TIPS
Top with any ingredients you like, for example:

- pitted olives, halved
- red onions, thinly sliced
- peppers, thinly sliced
- aubergine, salted to remove excess liquid and cooked
- goat's cheese, crumbled
- asparagus, sliced thinly
- mushrooms, sliced
- sliced meats, such as salami, pepperoni, chorizo, ham or chicken

DIY SAUSAGE ROLLS

A savoury bake that could not be easier! These are my go-to for so many occasions as they take little time to put together and are super versatile. Check out some of my favourite flavour combos in the tips section.

MAKES 6
PREP TIME 20 MINS
COOK TIME 25–30 MINS

1 roll puff pastry
500g of your favourite sausages (skins removed)
pinch of cracked black pepper
1 egg, beaten, for egg wash
2 tsp sesame seeds

To serve (optional)
relish or tomato ketchup

- Remove the puff pastry from the fridge 10–15 minutes before using. Preheat the oven to 200°C/180°C fan/gas mark 6. Line a baking tray with baking parchment.
- Remove the skins from your sausages and place the meat in a bowl. Add the pepper (or try the extra flavours in Gill's Tips) and mix.
- Unroll the sheet of puff pastry. Spoon your sausage mix into one big sausage down the centre of the pastry and brush the edges with egg wash. Fold the pastry over the sausage, and tuck it in nice and tightly. Cut off excess pastry at the sides (while keeping as much of a pastry tail as you like). Seal by crimping with a fork
- Cut the roll into six large sausage rolls (feel free to make smaller or larger ones). Brush each roll with egg wash and sprinkle the sesame seeds on top (I use a mix of black and white sesame seeds).
- Place on the baking tray, leaving enough space between them to expand. Bake for 25–30 minutes until nice and golden.
- Leave to cool on a wire rack for a few minutes. These are best eaten warm, but can be eaten cold. If reheating, do so in the oven until thoroughly hot.

 GILL'S TIPS
Here are some ideas for adding flavour: 2 tbsp honey and 2 tsp Dijon or wholegrain mustard; 100g uncooked black pudding, crumbled; approx. 1 tbsp spices, such as paprika, chilli powder, cumin, coriander or herbs, such as fresh or dried basil, oregano, thyme, sage; bacon/chorizo pieces; caramelised onions; grated cheese; replace the sausage meat with turkey, chicken or beef mince.

CHILLI BEEF EMPANADAS

✳ ✳ ✳

Pockets of buttery, flaky pastry filled with a spicy chilli beef and melty cheese. Make them ahead of time or bake them straight away for a DELICIOUS treat!

MAKES 15
PREP TIME 45 MINS
COOK TIME 55–60 MINS

Chilli
1 tbsp vegetable or olive oil
500g minced beef
1 white onion, peeled and diced small
1 red pepper, diced small
3 cloves garlic, peeled and minced
1 x 400g can chopped tomatoes
1 x 400g can kidney beans, drained and rinsed
60g tomato puree
1 beef stock pot or stock cube
1 tbsp light brown sugar
3 tsp smoked paprika
3 tsp ground cumin
3 tsp ground coriander
1 tsp oregano
1 tsp chilli powder
$1/2$ tsp chilli flakes
2 tsp Worcester sauce
salt and pepper

Chilli
- Put a large saucepan over a medium heat, add a tablespoon of vegetable oil and, when hot, add the mince. Stir often so that it doesn't stick. When it's nice and brown, add the onion, pepper and garlic. Cook for 5 minutes.
- Add in the rest of the chilli ingredients (add more chilli flakes if you like hot spice), bring to the boil, then reduce the heat and simmer for about 20 minutes, uncovered. Stir your chilli every few minutes to stop it catching on the bottom. Cook until nicely thickened (you want this mix thick and not too liquidy, as it has to be stuffed into pastry). Leave aside to cool completely.

Pastry
- While the chilli is cooling, make the pastry. Sift the flour and salt into a large bowl. Add the cubed, cold butter and rub it in until it resembles fine breadcrumbs.
- Add the milk and eggs, and mix until the dough forms.
- Bring together into a ball on a floured countertop with your hands. Wrap it tightly in cling film or baking parchment and refrigerate for at least 20 minutes.
- Preheat the oven to 200°C/180°C fan/gas mark 6 and line a large baking tray with baking parchment.
- Once the dough is chilled, roll out it on a floured surface to about 5mm thick. Then, using a round cutter or a small bowl approx. 10cm/4 inches in diameter, cut out 15 circles. You may need to bring the scraps back together and roll out again.

To combine
- Fill the centre of each round with a tablespoonful of the chilli and a sprinkle of grated cheese.

Pastry
400g plain flour
I tsp salt
200g unsalted butter,
   cubed and cold
50ml milk
2 eggs, beaten

Extras
150g cheddar cheese,
   grated
I egg, beaten, for egg
   wash
handful sesame seeds

- Brush the edges of the pastry circles with the egg wash, then fold the dough in half over the filling and crimp with a fork.
- Place the empanadas onto a baking tray. Brush with an egg wash and sprinkle with sesame seeds. Bake for 30–35 minutes until golden and crisp.
- Best eaten straight away but can be refrigerated and reheated in the oven.

 GILL'S TIPS

These empanadas can be cooked in a few different ways. I like to bake them or cook them in the air fryer but if you want to be super naughty you can deep-fry them too! I have included cooking times for the oven. They take about 15 minutes in the air fryer and 5–10 minutes in a deep-fat fryer.

SPINACH AND RICOTTA FILO PASTRY TARTS

Greek cuisine is one of my favourites, so I had to include a savoury pastry inspired by something I love: spanakopita, a Greek classic. This savoury spinach and cheese pie is something a little different as a starter dish or finger food option.

MAKES 6
PREP TIME 35 MINS
COOK TIME 30–35 MINS

1 roll of filo pastry
    (approx. 75g)
200g fresh spinach
60g feta cheese
80g ricotta cheese
1 clove garlic, peeled
    and minced
1 egg, beaten
1 tbsp finely chopped
    fresh parsley
1 tbsp finely chopped
    fresh dill
salt and pepper
25g salted butter,
    melted
1 egg, beaten, for egg
    wash
small handful of
    sesame seeds

- Remove the filo pastry from the fridge 10–15 minutes before it's needed. Preheat the oven to 180°C/160°C fan/gas mark 4. Lightly grease a cupcake tray with butter.
- Wilt the spinach in a bowl of boiling water, then drain and leave to cool. Once it is cool, squeeze it in a cloth to remove any excess water.
- Put the spinach in a bowl and add both cheeses, the garlic, egg and herbs, and season with salt and pepper. Mix until well combined and then place to one side.
- Unroll the sheets of filo pastry and cut them into 10 x 10cm (4 x 4 inch) squares. Each tart is made up of 4 squares for the base and 1 for the top, so you need 30 pieces.
- To assemble the tarts, take one square of filo pastry and brush with a small bit of melted butter. Take another square, layer it over the first piece at a slight angle and brush with butter. Repeat with another two pieces of filo, placing the pieces at an angle each time, to give a star-like shape.
- Lift up the filo star and press it into the cupcake tin to create a little cup. Repeat with the rest of the pastry to create 6 filo cups.
- Divide the cheesy spinach filling between the cups. Top each cup with a final square as a lid. Brush with the egg wash and sprinkle with sesame seeds.
- Bake for 30–35 minutes until golden. Allow to cool for a few minutes before removing from the tin. Eat immediately.

 GILL'S TIPS
Working with filo pastry can be tricky as it dries out fast. Covering your pastry with a damp tea towel while you shape the tarts will help!

MUFFINS/CUPCAKES

CHOCOLATE CHIP MUFFINS

I've found the perfect balance of oil and buttermilk to give you a deliciously moist chocolate muffin. A quick and easy recipe you will adore!

MAKES 10
PREP TIME 15 MINS
COOK TIME 25–30 MINS

100g salted butter, melted

300ml buttermilk

50ml vegetable oil

1 tsp vanilla extract

2 eggs

225g plain flour

55g cocoa powder

2 tsp baking powder

140g light brown sugar

40g caster sugar

200g mixed chocolate chips

- Preheat the oven to 200°C/180°C fan/gas mark 6. Place 10 muffin cases into a cupcake tin.
- Melt the butter in a heatproof bowl in the microwave in short bursts and allow it to cool a little. Add the buttermilk, oil, vanilla and eggs, and whisk.
- Into a separate bowl, sift the flour, cocoa powder and baking powder. Next mix in both the sugars. Make a well in the centre of the dry ingredients and pour in the wet ingredients.
- Whisk until just combined and then fold in the chocolate chips.
- Divide the mix evenly between the muffin cases. Top with extra chocolate chips if you wish!
- Bake for 25–30 minutes or until a toothpick or skewer comes out clean. Leave to cool.
- These will keep for up to three days in an airtight container. Enjoy!

GILL'S TIPS
Make your own tulip muffin cases by cutting squares of parchment paper and pushing them into a cupcake tin.

MOCHA MUFFINS

Chocolate and coffee? Probably one of the best combos! This is a rich, moist mocha sponge topped with a silky chocolate and coffee icing. For an added kick, make your espressos very strong!

MAKES 10
PREP TIME 30 MINS
COOK TIME 25–30 MINS

Muffins
200ml buttermilk
100ml cold espresso (or strong instant coffee)
50ml vegetable oil
100g unsalted butter, melted and cooled
2 eggs
1 tsp vanilla extract
225g plain flour
55g cocoa powder
2 tsp baking powder
pinch of salt
140g light brown sugar
40g caster sugar
200g mixed chocolate chips

Icing
120g unsalted butter
240g icing sugar
15g cocoa powder
50g dark chocolate, melted
6 tsp cold espresso (or strong instant coffee)

Optional decoration
10 coffee beans

- Preheat the oven to 200°C/180°C fan/gas mark 6. Place 10 muffin cases into a cupcake tin.
- In one bowl, whisk together the buttermilk, coffee, oil, melted butter, eggs and vanilla.
- Into a separate bowl, sift the flour, cocoa, baking powder and salt. Mix in both your sugars. Make a well in the centre of the dry ingredients and pour in the wet ingredients.
- Whisk until just combined and then fold in the chocolate chips.
- Spoon into the muffin cases evenly. Top with extra chocolate chips if you wish!
- Bake for 25–30 minutes or until a toothpick or skewer comes out clean. Leave to cool.
- Now let's make the icing: whisk the butter until pale and fluffy (using an electric whisk will give a smoother icing). Sift in the icing sugar and cocoa powder and whisk until well combined (begin at a low speed or the sugar will fly everywhere). Add the melted chocolate and whisk until well mixed.
- As you whisk, add the cooled espresso, one tablespoonful at a time, until the icing is a soft pipeable consistency.
- Smooth the icing on using a small spatula or pipe it on. If your icing bag is small, add in only half the icing at a time. Twist the end or tie a knot and then ice the muffin in one long squeeze, starting in the middle and slowly circling outwards, then up, to create a pretty swirl effect.
- Decorate each muffin with a coffee bean on top, if you like.
- These will keep for up to three days in an airtight container. Enjoy!

LEMON DRIZZLE MUFFINS

Lemon bakes have long been my mam's favourite – I have always been inspired by her when it comes to baking and I love to make a zesty bake whenever I can to surprise her.

MAKES 10
PREP TIME 30 MINS
COOK TIME 25–30 MINS

300ml buttermilk
100g unsalted butter,
   melted and cooled
50ml vegetable oil
2 eggs
280g plain flour
2 tsp baking powder
pinch of salt
140g light brown sugar
40g caster sugar
zest of a large lemon

Drizzle
50g caster sugar
50ml lemon juice

Icing
100g icing sugar
a few teaspoons of
   lemon juice

Topping
reserved lemon zest

- Preheat the oven to 200°C/180°C fan/gas mark 6. Place 10 muffin cases into a cupcake tin.
- In one bowl, whisk together the buttermilk, melted butter, oil and eggs.
- Into a separate bowl, sift the flour, baking powder and salt. Mix in both the sugars and then add the lemon zest (reserve some to use as topping).
- Make a well in the centre of the dry ingredients and pour in the wet ingredients. Whisk until just combined. Divide the mixture evenly between the muffin cases.
- Bake for 25–30 minutes or until a toothpick or skewer comes out clean. Allow to cool for 10 minutes.
- For the drizzle, mix the caster sugar and lemon juice until the sugar dissolves. With a spoon, drizzle the mixture over the muffins while they're still warm.
- For the icing, mix the icing sugar with enough lemon juice to reach your desired consistency: use less juice for a thick icing or more for a loose icing, adding a little at a time. Spoon the icing on top of the cooled muffins and top with the reserved lemon zest.
- These will keep for up to three days in an airtight container. Enjoy!

GILL'S TIPS
Swap the lemon with limes and swap 60g of the flour for shredded coconut for a tasty lime and coconut drizzle muffin. Top with some toasted flaked coconut for a tropical flavour.

TIRAMISU CUPCAKES

Love coffee and cake? All the flavours of a tiramisu popped in a cupcake! Think of the cupcake as the ladyfingers and the icing as the luscious tiramisu filling.
Creamy, punchy and sweet.

MAKES 12
PREP TIME 40 MINS
COOK TIME 18–20 MINS

Cupcake
175g unsalted butter
175g caster sugar
3 eggs
1 tsp vanilla extract
175g self-raising flour
pinch of salt
2 tsp milk

Coffee soak
50ml espresso (or
  strong instant coffee)
50g caster sugar

Buttercream
150g unsalted butter,
  at room temperature
150g icing sugar
1 tsp vanilla extract
275g mascarpone

Optional decoration
1 tbsp cocoa powder
12–24 coffee beans

- Preheat the oven to 180°C/160°C fan/gas mark 4. Line a cupcake tray with muffin cases.
- In a mixing bowl, cream together the butter and sugar until pale and fluffy. Add the eggs and vanilla and mix until combined.
- Sift the flour and salt into the mixture and gently fold. Next, fold in the milk to loosen the batter. Spoon the cupcake mix into the cupcake cases evenly.
- Bake for 18–20 minutes or until a toothpick or skewer comes out clean. Allow to cool.
- While the cupcakes are cooling, make the coffee soak. Mix the espresso and caster sugar in a bowl until the sugar is dissolved. Drizzle over the cooled cupcakes.
- Next is the buttercream: put the soft butter into a mixing bowl. Using an electric hand whisk, whip it up until very pale and fluffy. This will take about 5 minutes.
- Sift in the icing sugar, add the vanilla and whisk until incorporated well (begin at a low speed or the sugar will fly everywhere).
- Next, gently fold in the mascarpone cheese just until combined.
- Pipe a swirl onto your cupcakes and decorate with a dusting of cocoa powder and a coffee bean or two if you wish.
- These are best eaten on the same day but will keep in the fridge for two days.

 GILL'S TIPS
You can make the coffee soak as strong or as weak as you like.

STRAWBERRY WHITE CHOCOLATE MUFFINS

A super-moist and delicious muffin packed with strawberries and white chocolate chips. I love to make a batch of these muffins and deliver them to my friends and family, an all-round pleaser!

MAKES 10
PREP TIME 20 MINS
COOK TIME 25–30 MINS

300ml buttermilk

100g unsalted butter, melted and cooled

50ml vegetable oil

2 eggs

1 tsp vanilla extract

280g plain flour

2 tsp baking powder

pinch of salt

140g light brown sugar

40g caster sugar

125g white chocolate chips

120g strawberries, diced small

- Preheat the oven to 200°C/180°C fan/gas mark 6. Place 10 muffin cases into a cupcake tin.
- In one bowl, whisk together the buttermilk, melted butter, oil, eggs and vanilla.
- Into a separate bowl, sift the flour, baking powder and salt. Mix in both the sugars.
- Make a well in the centre of the dry ingredients and pour in the wet ingredients.
- Whisk until just combined and then fold in the white chocolate chips and the strawberries.
- Spoon the mixture into the muffin cases evenly. Top with some extra strawberries and white chocolate chips if you like.
- Bake for 25–30 minutes or until a toothpick or skewer comes out clean.
- Allow to cool.
- These will keep for up to three days in an airtight container. Enjoy!

GILL'S TIPS
Swap the white chocolate chips for dark or milk chocolate, if you prefer. You can also swap the strawberries for raspberries or blueberries.

STICKY TOFFEE CUPCAKES

MAKES 8
PREP TIME 45 MINS
COOK TIME 25–28 MINS

Cake
100g pitted dates
½ tsp bicarbonate of soda/baking soda
85ml hot water
2 tbsp treacle
60g unsalted butter
100g dark brown sugar
1 tsp vanilla extract
2 small eggs or 1 large
125g self-raising flour
¼ tsp salt
¼ tsp cinnamon
¼ tsp ground ginger
50g pecans, roughly chopped

Toffee sauce
300g light brown sugar
200ml single cream
150g salted butter
1 tbsp treacle

Buttercream
125g unsalted butter, at room temperature
250g icing sugar
⅛ tsp cinnamon
⅛ tsp ginger
½ tsp vanilla extract

To decorate
2 tbsp pecans, chopped small

- Put the dates, bicarbonate of soda and hot water in a bowl and leave to soak for 10–15 minutes. Blend in a food processor or mash with a fork (keeping the water in it). Stir in the treacle and set aside.
- Preheat the oven to 180°C/160°C fan/gas mark 4. Line a cupcake tray with cupcake cases.
- In a mixing bowl, cream together the butter and sugar until pale and fluffy. Whisk in the vanilla. Crack in the eggs and mix until well combined. Whisk in the blended date mix.
- Sift the flour, salt and spices into the mixture, add the chopped pecans and fold to combine.
- Divide the mixture evenly between the cupcake cases and bake for 25–28 minutes until a skewer comes out clean or the centre springs back when pressed. Leave to cool completely.
- Now for the toffee sauce: put all the ingredients into a saucepan over a medium heat and bring to the boil. Then reduce the heat and simmer until slightly thickened and darkened. (This will take only a few minutes.) Set aside to cool.
- Next, make the buttercream. Put the soft butter into a mixing bowl. Using an electric hand whisk, whip it up until very pale and fluffy. This will take about 5 minutes.
- Sift in the icing sugar in 2 separate batches and whisk until incorporated well (begin at a low speed or the sugar will fly everywhere). Mix in the spices and vanilla. Next, mix in enough toffee sauce to give a silky pipeable icing (about 75g).
- Now assemble the cupcakes. Using an apple corer or a knife, make a shallow hole in the top of each cupcake. Drizzle in some toffee sauce. Pipe buttercream on top and then drizzle with some more sauce and a sprinkle of chopped nuts.
- These will keep for up to three days in an airtight container.

DARK CHOCOLATE BLACKBERRY CUPCAKES

A rich chocolate cupcake filled with a tangy blackberry jam and topped with a silky-smooth vanilla and blackberry buttercream: a beautiful cupcake with a fun twist on flavour.

MAKES 12
PREP TIME 35 MINS
COOK TIME 20–25 MINS

Cupcake
115g dark chocolate
115g unsalted butter
90g plain flour
15g cocoa powder
1 tsp baking powder
1/8 tsp bicarbonate of
  soda/baking soda
pinch of salt
100g light brown sugar
80g of caster sugar
60ml buttermilk
2 eggs
1 tsp vanilla extract

Buttercream
170g unsalted butter,
  at room temperature
340g icing sugar
100g blackberry jam

Extras
12 tsp blackberry jam
1 punnet blackberries
2 tbsp grated dark
  chocolate

- Preheat the oven to 180°C/160°C fan/gas mark 4. Line a 12-cup muffin tray with cupcake cases.
- Melt the dark chocolate and butter together in a heatproof bowl in the microwave, stirring regularly.
- Sift the flour, cocoa powder, baking powder, bicarbonate of soda and salt into a bowl. Add in both sugars and mix.
- In a separate bowl, whisk together the buttermilk, eggs and vanilla.
- Make a well in the dry ingredients, pour in the wet ingredients and the chocolate mix and stir until well incorporated.
- Divide the mixture evenly between the cupcake cases. An ice-cream scoop is ideal for this. Bake in the oven for 20–25 minutes and then leave to cool completely.
- While the cupcakes are baking, make the buttercream. Put the soft butter into a mixing bowl. Whisk until very pale and fluffy. This will take about 5 minutes with an electric hand whisk.
- Sift in the icing sugar in 3 separate batches and whisk until incorporated well (begin at a low speed or the sugar will fly everywhere).
- Next, add the blackberry jam and continue whisking.
- When the cupcakes are cool, using an apple corer or knife, cut a hole in each one, going about halfway down. Fill up each cupcake with a teaspoonful of blackberry jam.
- Pipe the buttercream on top of each cupcake and then garnish with some fresh blackberries and grated chocolate.
- These will keep for up to three days in an airtight container.

LEMON BLUEBERRY CUPCAKES

A zesty cupcake with pops of juicy blueberries, topped with a silky buttercream and a dollop of fresh homemade blueberry jam. A gorgeous bake for a delicious summer party dessert!

MAKES 12
PREP TIME 35 MINS
COOK TIME 18–20 MINS

Cupcake
175g unsalted butter
175g caster sugar
3 eggs
zest of 1 lemon
175g self-raising flour
pinch of salt
2 tbsp of milk
85g blueberries

Jam
250g fresh or frozen
  blueberries
100g caster sugar
zest of half a lemon

Buttercream
160g unsalted butter,
  at room temperature
320g icing sugar
zest of half a lemon
1 tbsp blueberry jam
a few drops of milk

- Preheat the oven to 180°C/160°C fan/gas mark 4. Line the cupcake tray with cupcake cases.
- In a mixing bowl, cream together the butter and sugar until pale and fluffy. Add the eggs and lemon zest and whisk until combined. Sift the flour and salt into the mix and gently fold. Fold in the milk to loosen the batter slightly.
- Spoon the cupcake mix evenly into your cupcake cases. Place about 3 blueberries into each cupcake and press lightly into the batter.
- Bake for 18–20 minutes or until a toothpick or skewer comes out clean. Leave to cool completely.
- While your cupcakes are baking, make the jam. Place the blueberries, caster sugar and lemon zest into a pot over a medium heat and bring to the boil, then reduce to a low heat and simmer for 5–10 minutes until thickened.
- Spread the jam into a large baking dish and put it into the fridge to cool quickly.
- Next, make the buttercream: place the soft butter in a mixing bowl. Using an electric hand whisk, whip it up until very pale and fluffy. This will take about 5 minutes.
- Sift in the icing sugar in 3 separate batches and mix until incorporated well (begin at a low speed or the sugar will fly everywhere).
- Add in the lemon zest and blueberry jam and whisk. For a lovely pipeable consistency, add a few drops of milk until you have a silky buttercream.

Optional decoration
a few pinches of lemon
zest
handful of fresh
blueberries

- Pipe the buttercream onto the cupcakes (I use a star nozzle). Start by piping in the middle, circling out and then up.
- Top with a generous teaspoonful of your homemade blueberry jam.
- Finish with some fresh lemon zest for a pop of colour and some fresh blueberries, if you wish.
- These will keep for up to three days in an airtight container.

 GILL'S TIPS

You can swap the blueberries in these cupcakes for raspberries or blackberries instead.

NO-BAKE TREATS

CHOCOLATE TRUFFLES

A creamy chocolate ganache truffle coated in chocolate flakes. A perfect gift for yourself or packaged up as a homemade gift, with your favourite truffle flavours.
Easily adapted to your taste!

MAKES 15
PREP TIME 3 HOURS
APPROX.

**125g dark chocolate,
broken into squares**
**100g milk chocolate,
broken into squares**
150ml single cream
15g salted butter
**2 tbsp chocolate
shavings**

- Put all the chocolate, cream and butter in a medium-sized heatproof bowl and melt in short blasts in the microwave, stirring regularly. Place the mixture into the fridge to set until firm. (This will take a couple of hours.)
- Line a tray with parchment paper.
- Remove the ganache mixture from the fridge. Roll it into 15 balls and place them onto the parchment paper. Set these in the fridge for a further 30 minutes or so to firm up.
- Once firm, dip each truffle in chocolate shavings or your coating of choice and roll until covered. Place back on the tray and return them to the fridge for 20 minutes. They should set fairly quickly but best to be safe.
- Store in the fridge until eating. Enjoy!

 GILL'S TIPS
Here are some coating ideas (you'll need a few tablespoonfuls of each):

- roasted nuts, chopped very small
- freeze-dried fruit
- desiccated coconut
- cocoa powder, sieved onto a plate
- 200g melted chocolate

COOKIES AND CREAM FUDGE

This is one of the easiest recipes I have ever made: it looks very impressive yet it's oh so simple! Only a handful of ingredients are needed to make this delicious treat – a blast of cookies and cream in one bite.

MAKES 16 PIECES
PREP TIME 2 HOURS 20
MINS

**1 tin condensed milk
(397 g)
475g white chocolate,
broken into pieces
1 tsp vanilla extract
2 packets of cookies
and cream biscuits
(approx. 300g in
total)**

- Grease a 20 x 20cm (8 x 8 inch) baking tin and then line with baking parchment.
- In a large heatproof bowl, put the condensed milk, white chocolate and vanilla and melt gently in a bain-marie (see page 11).
- While the mix is melting, roughly crush your biscuits in a separate bowl with a rolling pin (we want pieces of different sizes, not fine crumbs).
- Once the mixture has melted, add in three quarters of the crushed biscuits. (The remainder will be for decoration.) Gently fold in the biscuits, then spoon the mix onto the baking tray and smooth it down with a spatula. Crush the remaining biscuits more finely and sprinkle over the fudge mix.
- Place the tray in the fridge for at least 2 hours to set firmly. To slice up, heat a knife in a mug of hot water for a nice sharp cut.
- This will keep for up to two weeks in an airtight container.

 GILL'S TIPS
- Use any biscuits or chocolate you like for different flavours.
- Bag up and give this a tasty gift!

MINI WHITE CHOCOLATE CHEESECAKES

A quick and easy dessert that needs no baking! You can tailor it to your taste by using your favourite type of chocolate.

MAKES 2 LARGE OR 4 SMALL CHEESECAKES
PREP TIME 30 MINS

60g white chocolate
75g digestive biscuits
30g unsalted butter, melted
160g cream cheese
60g icing sugar
75ml single cream
½ tsp vanilla extract

To serve
a medium-sized hollow Easter egg, halved, or 4 small ramekins

Decorations
a handful of grated chocolate, mini Easter eggs, broken-up chocolate bars, chocolate buttons or any of your favourite treats

- In a heatproof bowl, melt the chocolate in short blasts in the microwave, stirring at regular intervals. Set aside to cool.
- Crush the biscuits in a bowl (or Ziploc bag) with a rolling pin to the texture of fine breadcrumbs. Mix in the melted butter. Divide the mixture between the Easter egg halves or ramekins and gently flatten down.
- Place the cream cheese and icing sugar in a small mixing bowl and whisk till smooth (begin at a low speed or the sugar will fly everywhere).
- Add the cream and vanilla. Whisk until slightly thickened.
- Add in the melted and cooled white chocolate, and whisk just until combined.
- Divide this cheesecake mixture between your four ramekins or two Easter egg halves and smooth over.
- Now for the fun part! Decorate these beauties however you like (or keep them simple).
- Serve straight away or keep chilled until serving.

GILL'S TIPS
These mini cheesecakes can be made in any dish you have in the kitchen. I LOVE making them at Easter using chocolate eggs as my serving dish!

CHOCOLATE MOUSSE

Make these in advance for a luxury chocolatey dessert. For more servings, simply multiply the recipe.

SERVES 2
PREP TIME 2 HOURS 20 MINS

175g dark chocolate, broken into pieces
30g salted butter
3 egg whites
30g caster sugar

To serve
fresh cream, whipped
grated chocolate

- Set two serving glasses aside.
- In a heatproof bowl, melt the chocolate and butter in the microwave in short bursts, and leave aside to cool.
- Whisk the egg whites until they form soft peaks. (It's best to use an electric whisk.) Add the sugar a spoonful at a time, whisking continuously, until the mixture forms stiff glossy peaks.
- Fold the melted chocolate/butter into the egg mixture very carefully until no streaks appear, being careful not to deflate the egg whites.
- Spoon into the serving glasses and then refrigerate for at least two hours.
- Top with some whipped cream and some grated chocolate if you like, and serve.

 GILL'S TIPS
- Because this recipe calls for raw egg whites, it's best to use the pasteurised version, which is available, bottled, in most supermarkets.
- Add in some orange zest for zingy flavour or chopped nuts for some texture. Save the unused egg yolks for my delicious crème brûlée tart recipe (see page 187)!

CHOCOLATE BISCUIT CAKE

This classic recipe is one of the most popular with my followers. This time we are going to keep it simple but check out the other flavour options in my tips!

MAKES 16 PIECES
PREP TIME 4 HOURS 30 MINS

220g dark chocolate, broken into pieces
220g milk chocolate, broken into pieces
220g salted butter, cubed
220g condensed milk
125g Rich Tea biscuits, roughly crushed
125g digestive biscuits, roughly crushed
100g Maltesers or malted milk balls
100g Crunchie bars or chocolate honeycomb bars, roughly chopped

- Grease a 20 x 20cm (8 x 8 inch) baking tin (or any tin/mould you like) and line with baking parchment.
- In a bain-marie (see page 11), heat the chocolate and butter until nearly melted. Be careful not to let this mixture get hot at all. Remove it from the heat while there are still a few small chunks and mix until smooth.
- Next, pour in the condensed milk. Fold through very gently until just combined. It will take only a few seconds. (It's fine if there are a few streaks as it will be mixed again with the filling. Over-mixing it may cause it to separate.)
- Add in the crushed biscuits, Maltesers and Crunchie bars, and fold through just until everything is coated.
- Pour the mixture into the lined tray and flatten down, pressing to make sure there are no gaps or air bubbles. To get the top as flat as possible, give the tray a jiggle and press down with a spatula. Place in the fridge to set for at least 4 hours.
- Once set, remove your biscuit cake from the tin and slice it with a warmed knife. Enjoy!

 GILL'S TIPS

Change up your biscuits and chocolate bars to any of your favourites, for example:

Bars	Biscuits	Other
Cadbury Caramel	Biscoff	marshmallows
Mars or Snickers	custard creams	nuts
KitKat	bourbon biscuits	dried fruit

COOKIE DOUGH BITES

We all love cookie dough, but unfortunately it isn't safe to eat. This recipe is made to be eaten and enjoyed raw. A quick and easy cookie dough fix!

MAKES 16
PREP TIME 1 HOUR 45
MINS

125g plain flour
55g unsalted butter
50g light brown sugar
30g caster sugar
25ml milk
1 tsp vanilla extract
50g milk chocolate
   chips
80g milk chocolate,
   melted

- Line a baking tray with baking parchment.
- Put the flour into a heatproof bowl and microwave for 30–60 seconds until hot throughout (this is to kill any bacteria). Leave to cool completely (about 20 minutes).
- In a large mixing bowl, cream together the butter and both sugars until light and fluffy.
- Add the milk and vanilla and combine until smooth.
- Sift in the flour and add the chocolate chips. Fold until you have a firm dough.
- Roll the dough into 16 even balls between your fingers – around 20g each – and place on the lined tray.
- Melt the chocolate in a heatproof bowl in the microwave in short blasts, then drizzle it over the cookie dough bites.
- Refrigerate for about an hour until set.
- Once set, store in a sealed container in the fridge. They will keep up to a week.
- Enjoy!

 GILL'S TIPS
Make your cookie dough balls smaller and mix them through ice cream!

PEANUT CARAMEL CRUNCHY SQUARES

Smooth salted caramel topped with a layer of milk chocolate marbled with peanut butter on a crunchy base – peanut HEAVEN!

MAKES 9 LARGE BARS OR
18 MEDIUM
PREP TIME 2 HOURS 40
MINS

Base
125g unsalted butter
**500g Snickers bars or
    similar, chopped up
    into small pieces**
**150g Rice Krispies (or
    similar)**

Caramel
150g salted butter
150g light brown sugar
**1 tin condensed milk
    (397g)**
2 tbsp golden syrup
1 tsp vanilla extract

Toppings
300g milk chocolate
1 tbsp peanut butter
**2 Snickers bars (or
    similar – 100g
    approx.), thinly sliced**

- Grease a 20 x 20cm (8 x 8 inch) baking tin and line with parchment.
- In a bain-marie (see page 11), melt the butter and Snickers bars until smooth. This will take about 10 minutes. (The butter can separate from the nougat and chocolate, but if you remove from the heat and stir quickly, they will combine together.)
- Take off the heat and quickly fold in the Rice Krispies until fully incorporated. Work fast as the mixture will set quite rapidly.
- Tip the mixture into the tin and flatten down evenly. Leave to set in the fridge for 15 minutes.
- For the caramel layer, put all the ingredients in a saucepan and place on a medium heat. Using a spatula, continually mix to make sure it doesn't catch at the bottom.
- Bring to a boil and boil for 5 minutes while stirring continually. Set a timer to get your caramel perfect! When it's ready, the mixture will thicken and darken.
- Pour this caramel directly on top of the cooled base layer. Smooth it out flat – please mind your fingers as the mixture is incredibly hot! – then refrigerate until cool (which will take about 2 hours).
- Once the caramel has cooled, melt the milk chocolate in a heatproof bowl in quick bursts in the microwave, and then pour on top. Smooth over until flat. Give the tray a jiggle to level the chocolate.

- Warm the peanut butter in the microwave, and then drizzle on top. Feather with a skewer, if you like.
- Finally, top with slivers of Snickers bars.
- Leave to set in the fridge until firm, then cut with a warmed sharp knife into 9 large or 18 medium pieces.
- These will keep fresh for up to three days in an airtight container. Enjoy!

 GILL'S TIPS

Please be very careful when making the caramel as it is a very hot mixture. Do not touch or taste it while hot and be sure to protect your fingers.

TRAYBAKES

THE ULTIMATE BROWNIES

These brownies are on a whole new level with extra layers of flavour to intensify that luxurious brownie taste. The only brownie recipe you need!

MAKES 9
PREP TIME 2 HOURS 30 MINS
COOK TIME 25–30 MINS

185g unsalted butter
125g dark chocolate, broken into pieces
185g light brown sugar
160g caster sugar
2 large eggs + 1 egg yolk
2 tbsp espresso (or strong coffee)
1 tsp vanilla extract
125g plain flour
75g cocoa powder
½ tsp salt
85g milk chocolate chips
85g dark chocolate chips

- Melt the butter in a small saucepan over a medium heat. Let it boil until you see the milk solids sink to the bottom and it turns a nice golden-brown colour. Remove from the heat and pour into a clean bowl. Let it cool for 5 minutes.
- Mix the dark chocolate into the butter and stir until smooth.
- Preheat the oven to 200°C/180°C fan/gas mark 6. Line a 20 x 20cm (8 x 8 inch) tin with baking parchment.
- Make up an espresso or strong coffee and allow it to cool.
- Put the sugar, eggs and egg yolk in a bowl and whisk until light and fluffy. Add in the chocolate/butter mix and whisk again. Next, mix in the coffee and vanilla.
- Sift in the flour, cocoa powder and salt and fold. Next, add all the chocolate chips and gently fold.
- Pour into your prepared tin and smooth out with a spatula.
- Bake for 25–30 minutes (there will still be a slight jiggle in the centre when it's done). Allow it to cool at room temperature and refrigerate for about two hours until cold. (This will ensure you get super-nice cuts on your gooey brownies.)
- Once it is chilled, warm a sharp knife in a mug of hot water and cut into 9 pieces. Clean the knife between each cut.
- These will keep for up to a week in an airtight container, and are delicious reheated in the microwave!

 GILL'S TIPS
Make your brownies extra luxurious by adding in some chopped nuts with the chocolate chips, e.g. macadamia nuts, hazelnuts, pecans, walnuts, etc.

BAKEWELL SLICE

A bakewell is one of the first cakes I remember eating. My nana always had them in the house and I was addicted to that almond flavour. The mini tarts are quite fiddly to make so I tried it out as a traybake and I am OBSESSED with it!

MAKES 12
PREP TIME 1 HOUR 45 MINS
COOK TIME 50 MINS

Pastry
150g plain flour
50g unsalted butter
approx. 50ml cold
water

Cake
150g unsalted butter
150g caster sugar
3 eggs
½ tsp almond extract
75g ground almonds
75g self-raising flour
½ tsp baking powder
pinch of salt

100g raspberry jam
handful of flaked
almonds

Drizzle
4 tbsp icing sugar
a few teaspoons water

- Preheat the oven to 200°C/180°C fan/gas mark 6. Grease and line a 20 x 20cm (8 x 8 inch) square tin.
- For the pastry base, sift the flour into a bowl and rub in the butter until you have a breadcrumb-like consistency. Add in just enough water to form a dough. Be careful not to over-mix it.
- Roll out the pastry on a floured surface to the size of the base of your tin and place it in the tin. Use your fingers to get it neat and level.
- Bake for 10–15 minutes until a light golden brown, then set aside to cool.
- For the cake layer, cream together the butter and sugar in a large bowl until light and fluffy. Add the eggs and almond extract and whisk through. Fold in the ground almonds, sift in the flour, baking powder and salt, and mix until just combined.
- Grab the baking tin and spread the jam over the cooked pastry. Pour the cake batter on top and smooth it over evenly. Top with some flaked almonds.
- Bake for 30–35 minutes until the centre of the cake is cooked. (To check if it is done, poke in a skewer: if it comes out clean, the cake is baked. Or if you press the centre, it should spring back.) Leave to cool completely (about an hour).
- Once cooled, remove the cake from the tin and cut into as many pieces (or whatever shape) you like! I cut mine in 12.
- To make the drizzle, simply mix the icing sugar with a few drops of water. Add as much or as little water as you like depending on how loose you like your drizzle. For an extra almondy kick, add a few drops of almond extract.
- Grab a slice and enjoy!

WHITE CHOCOLATE RASPBERRY BLONDIES

A white chocolate version of a brownie, packed with white chocolate chips and fresh raspberries. Gooey white chocolate heaven!

MAKES 9
PREP TIME I HOUR 40 MINS
COOK TIME 30–38 MINS

170g unsalted butter, cubed

200g light brown sugar

80g caster sugar

2 eggs

1 tsp vanilla extract

250g plain flour

pinch of salt

125g white chocolate chips

100g fresh raspberries

- Preheat the oven to 180°C/160°C fan/gas mark 4. Grease a 20 x 20cm (8 x 8 inch) square tin and line with parchment.
- Put the butter and both sugars in a bowl and whisk together until light and fluffy.
- Next, whisk in the eggs, one at a time, and then whisk in the vanilla.
- Once combined, sift in the flour and salt and gently fold. Fold in the white chocolate chips.
- Spoon half of the mixture into a baking tin and smooth down with a spatula. Layer on the fresh raspberries and then spoon the remaining blondie mix on top and smooth out very gently.
- Bake for 30–38 minutes (they will be set on top with a slight jiggle in the middle when done). Allow to cool completely (this will take about an hour). If you can bear to wait a while longer, putting it in the fridge when cool for a further few minutes will give you super-sharp cuts when you slice it up.
- These will keep for up to three days in an airtight container.

 GILL'S TIPS

Want to play with other blondie flavours? Change up the chocolate percentage of your chips, replace the raspberries with 100g chopped-up chocolate bars, biscuits, nuts, dried fruit, or add the zest of an orange, lemon or lime for some fun flavours!

RED VELVET TRAYBAKE CAKE

A super-soft velvety sponge with a gorgeous cocoa and vanilla flavour, topped with a silky cream cheese icing. Red velvet cake will always be one of my favourites!

MAKES 9
PREP TIME 1 HOUR 40 MINS
COOK TIME 30–35 MINS

Cake
100g unsalted butter
150g caster sugar
1 egg
1 tsp vanilla extract
1 tsp red gel colouring
120ml buttermilk
1 tsp white vinegar
165g plain flour
5g cocoa powder
1 tsp bicarbonate of
 soda/baking soda
½ tsp salt

Icing
100g unsalted butter,
 at room temperature
100g icing sugar
225g cream cheese
1 tsp vanilla extract

- Preheat the oven to 180°C/160°C fan/gas mark 4. Grease a 20 x 20cm (8 x 8 inch) square tin and line with baking parchment.
- In a mixing bowl, cream together the butter and sugar together until pale and fluffy. Add the egg, vanilla and red gel colouring and mix.
- Next add the buttermilk and vinegar, and whisk. The mixture will look very wet but that's normal.
- Sift in the flour, cocoa, bicarbonate of soda and salt. Fold through until just combined. Do not over-mix.
- Pour into your baking tin and bake for 30–35 minutes, or until a toothpick or skewer comes out clean. Leave to cool completely (this will take about an hour).
- Now for the icing: in a mixing bowl, whisk the butter until pale and fluffy. Sift in the icing sugar and whisk well (begin at a low speed or the sugar will fly everywhere).
- Add the cream cheese and vanilla. Whisk until fully combined.
- Once the cake has cooled completely, slice a thin layer off the top – you need just the smallest sliver to crumble on top of the icing.
- Spread the icing evenly with a spatula on top of the cake. Top with the cake crumbs and slice up!
- This will keep for up to three days in an airtight container.

 GILL'S TIPS

It's best to use a red food gel when baking as the liquid ones never give the correct colour needed for red velvet cake. Food gel colours are very strong and are easily available in supermarkets or online.

MILLIONAIRE'S SHORTBREAD

The classic millionaire's shortbread we all know and love: a soft buttery base with a thick layer of delicious caramel topped with a layer of chocolate.

MAKES 9
PREP TIME 3 HOURS 45
  MINS
COOK TIME 40 MINS

Base
240g plain flour
**180g salted butter, cold
  and cubed**
90g caster sugar
¼ tsp vanilla extract

Caramel
150g salted butter
150g light brown sugar
**1 tin condensed milk
  (397g)**
2 tbsp golden syrup
1 tsp vanilla extract

Topping
**150g dark chocolate,
  broken into pieces**
**150g milk chocolate,
  broken into pieces**

- Preheat the oven to 180°C/160°C fan/gas mark 4. Grease a 20 x 20cm (8 x 8 inch) baking tin and line with baking parchment.
- Sift the flour into a mixing bowl. Rub in the cubed butter till you have a breadcrumb-like consistency. Add the sugar and vanilla and mix. This will still look very crumbly but that's OK. Tip the mixture into your prepared tin and flatten it down until it's nice and even. Bake for 20–25 minutes until lightly golden on top. Set aside to cool.
- Put all the caramel ingredients into a saucepan and set it over a medium heat. Bring to the boil, mixing continually to make sure it doesn't burn at the bottom. Boil for 5 minutes while stirring constantly. Set a timer to get it perfect! Your mixture will thicken and darken when it's ready. Please mind your fingers because it is incredibly hot!
- Pour the mixture directly onto the shortbread layer. Smooth it out flat and then put it in the fridge until cool (this will take about two hours).
- In a heatproof bowl, melt the chocolate in short blasts in the microwave, stirring regularly, and then pour on top of the cooled caramel. Smooth out until even and then refrigerate until firm (about an hour).
- When it is fully cool, heat up a knife in a mug of hot water and cut your bake into squares.
- These will keep for up to a week in an airtight container.

CARAMEL CORNFLAKE BROWNIES

Want an over-the-top bake? Here it is! Two indulgent layers to make one epic bake.

MAKES 9
PREP TIME 2 HOURS 45
 MINS
COOK TIME 30 MINS

Brownie
**140g unsalted butter,
 cubed**
**100g dark chocolate,
 broken into pieces**
2 eggs
300g caster sugar
100g plain flour
60g cocoa powder
**150g milk chocolate
 chips**

Caramel
350g caster sugar
200ml single cream
**100g salted butter,
 cubed**
160g cornflakes

- Preheat the oven to 200°C/180°C fan/gas mark 6. Grease a 20 x 20cm (8 x 8 inch) baking tin and line with baking parchment.
- In a heatproof bowl, melt the butter and chocolate in short blasts in the microwave, stirring regularly. Leave to cool for a few minutes.
- Put the eggs and sugar in a bowl and whisk until fluffy. Add in the chocolate and butter mix and whisk until well combined. Sift in the flour and cocoa, and fold until just combined, then fold in the chocolate chips.
- Pour the mixture into the baking tray and spread it nice and flat. Bake for approximately 30 minutes. There will still be a slight jiggle in the centre of your brownies. Leave to cool completely and then refrigerate.
- For the caramel, put the sugar in a medium saucepan over a low heat. Cook, without stirring, until the sugar caramelises and goes a light amber colour (stirring can move sugar to the sides of the saucepan where it may crystallise.)
- Mix in the cream. Be careful as this bubbles and lets off a lot of heat. Once combined, remove from the heat. Keep stirring and add the butter a cube at a time.
- Place back on the heat and cook for a further 5 minutes approximately while continuously stirring. Cook until the mixture thickens slightly.
- Mix in the cornflakes and then pour over the brownie. Flatten down nice and firmly.
- Place in the fridge until completely cold (about 2 hours). Portion up your brownies and enjoy!
- They will keep for up to a week in an airtight container.

CARAMEL COOKIE BARS

*

You can't go wrong with this traybake. A gooey, crispy cookie dough packed with milk chocolate chips and a surprise caramel layer – DELICIOUS!

MAKES 9
PREP TIME I HOUR 30 MINS
COOK TIME 20 MINS

145g salted butter, at room temperature

125g light brown sugar

75g caster sugar

2 small eggs

I tsp vanilla extract

325g plain flour

2 tbsp cornflour

½ tsp baking powder

½ tsp bicarbonate of soda/baking soda

225g chocolate chips

225g Carnation caramel (or similar)

Optional

a large pinch of sea salt

a small handful of chocolate chips

- Preheat the oven to 200°C/180°C fan/gas mark 6. Grease a 20 x 20cm (8 x 8 inch) baking tin and line with baking parchment.
- In a large mixing bowl, cream the butter and both sugars together until light and fluffy. Add in the eggs and vanilla, and whisk until well combined.
- Sift in the flour, cornflour, baking powder and bicarbonate of soda and fold until it forms a dough. Fold through the chocolate chips.
- Place half the mixture in the lined dish and flatten down. Spread the caramel over this and then top with the rest of the dough. Sprinkle on extra chocolate chips and sea salt, if you like.
- Bake for 20 minutes until nicely browned on top.
- Leave to cool completely and then place in the fridge until cold. This will give you a lovely sharp cut.
- Cut into 9 generous squares. Heat up to serve or eat at room temperature. They are amazing warmed up and served with a scoop of vanilla ice cream!

 GILL'S TIPS

Swap out the caramel for your favourite sauce or spreads, for example:

- raspberry jam with white chocolate chips
- peanut butter and chopped peanuts
- chocolate hazelnut spread and chopped hazelnuts

APPLE CRUMBLE TRAYBAKE CAKE

A soft spiced sponge with pockets of sweet apple, topped with a crunchy buttery crumble.
Top with some cream or custard for a delicious dessert!

SERVES 9
PREP TIME 1 HOUR 15 MINS
COOK TIME 35–45 MINS

Cake
175g unsalted butter
85g caster sugar
85g light brown sugar
1 tsp vanilla extract
3 eggs
175g self-raising flour
½ tsp cinnamon
pinch of salt

Apple
350g cooking apples,
   peeled and diced
65g sugar

Crumble
125g plain flour
65g light brown sugar
65g unsalted butter

- Preheat the oven to 180°C/160°C fan/gas mark 4. Grease a 20 x 20cm (8 x 8 inch) tin and line with baking parchment.
- In a mixing bowl, cream together the butter and both sugars until pale and fluffy. Add the vanilla, and then mix in the eggs, one at a time.
- Sift in the flour, cinnamon and salt, and fold until combined. Spoon the mixture into the tin and smooth down.
- In a separate bowl, mix together the diced apple and sugar. Sprinkle this over the cake batter.
- Now for the crumble: put the flour and sugar in a bowl. Rub in the butter until it resembles breadcrumbs. Sprinkle this crumble mix over the apples.
- Bake for 35–45 minutes or until a toothpick or skewer comes out clean and the cake springs back when gently pressed.
- Leave to cool completely (about 45 minutes) or serve warm with some ice cream, fresh cream or custard.

 GILL'S TIPS

Any apples will work for this recipe. I prefer cooking apples and they melt into the cake and soften up slightly more than eating apples.

RASPBERRY SWIRL CHEESECAKE BARS

A smooth, creamy, zesty cheesecake bar swirled with sweet raspberry coulis on top of a buttery biscuit base. The homemade coulis is a game changer for me!

MAKES 9
PREP TIME 1 HOUR 40 MINS
COOK TIME 40–45 MINS

Raspberry coulis
150g raspberries
40g caster sugar

Base
250g digestive biscuits
120g salted butter

Filling
50g plain flour
450g cream cheese
 (full fat)
100ml double cream
100g caster sugar
2 eggs
1 tsp vanilla extract
zest and juice of half a
 lemon

- For the coulis, put the raspberries and sugar in a saucepan over a medium heat. Bring to a boil, then reduce the heat and simmer for about 5 minutes. Pour into a bowl and allow to cool. When it is cooled, strain the coulis through a sieve, then set aside.
- Preheat the oven to 200°C/180°C fan/gas mark 6. Grease a 20 x 20cm (8 x 8 inch) tin and line with baking parchment.
- Crush the digestives to a fine crumb in a food processor or in a Ziploc bag using a rolling pin. In a heatproof bowl in the microwave, melt the butter and add it to the crumbs. Mix until well combined. Press the mix into the tin and then place in the freezer for 10–15 minutes until solid.
- While the base is setting, make the cheesecake. Sift the flour into a big mixing bowl and add all the filling ingredients. Whisk until well combined. Pour this mixture on top of the biscuit base and smooth over until level.
- Drizzle your raspberry coulis over it and then swirl through very gently with a knife or skewer.
- Place in the oven and bake for 40–45 minutes until the sides are set but centre still has a slight wobble.
- Leave to cool at room temperature and then place in the fridge until completely cold (about an hour). Portion up into 9 bars (but feel free to cut them smaller if you prefer).
- These will keep in the fridge for up to three days.

GILL'S TIPS
Swap the raspberries for a different fruit to change up the flavour, or simply leave them out for a classic baked cheesecake bar.

CAKES

VANILLA FUNFETTI BIRTHDAY CAKE

As a child, I DREAMED of a bright and colourful cake like this!
A classic vanilla cake, it's perfect for any celebration or special occasion.

SERVES 12
PREP TIME 3 HOURS
COOK TIME 32–40 MINS

Cake
225g unsalted butter,
**   at room temperature**
225g caster sugar
4 eggs
2 tsp vanilla extract
225g self-raising flour
pinch of salt
3 tbsp sprinkles

Buttercream
250g unsalted butter,
**   at room temperature**
500g icing sugar
2 tsp vanilla extract
2–4 tsp milk

Filling
6 tbsp raspberry jam

Funfetti
100g sprinkles

- Preheat the oven to 180°C/160°C fan/gas mark 4. Grease and line the base of two 15cm (6 inch) cake tins.
- In a mixing bowl, cream together the butter and sugar until pale and fluffy. Add the eggs and vanilla and mix until combined. Sift the flour and salt into the mixture and gently fold. Add the sprinkles and fold again.
- Divide the mixture evenly between the two baking tins and bake for 32–40 minutes until a toothpick or skewer comes out clean or the centre of the sponge springs back when pressed. Cool in the tins for 15 minutes, then remove the cakes to a wire rack to cool completely (about two hours).
- Once completely cooled, take a sliver off the top of each sponge if necessary to make them flat.
- While the cakes are cooling, make the buttercream. Put the soft butter into a mixing bowl and, using an electric hand whisk, whip it up until very pale and fluffy. This will take about 5 minutes. Sift in the icing sugar in three separate batches, whisking until incorporated well (begin at a low speed or the sugar will fly everywhere).
- Mix in the vanilla. Add the milk one teaspoonful at a time until the mixture reaches a nice spreadable consistency.
- Spread a small bit of buttercream on a serving board or plate. Place one layer of sponge on this. Pipe a border of buttercream around the top of the sponge. Fill the centre with 2 tablespoons of jam. Top the jam with more buttercream, making sure to get this nice and level. Top with the other layer of cake. (Tip: flip the upper layer of cake and use the base for a smoother top.)

- Refrigerate for about 20 minutes for the buttercream to firm up.
- Now it's time to do a crumb coat. Apply a very thin and smooth layer of buttercream all around your cake using a palette knife. Place it back in the fridge for about 20 minutes until firm to touch.
- Next, apply a thick coating of buttercream all around the cake. Using a cake scraper or a palette knife, smooth until you get a nice finish. Cover your cake with loads of sprinkles: take a handful and gently press them to the sides until the cake is completely covered. Do this over a clean countertop or a large bowl so you can collect any fallen sprinkles to use again.
- Refrigerate for 20 minutes to set.
- This cake will keep for up to three days in an airtight container – if it lasts that long!

 GILL'S TIPS

- When mixing dry ingredients for a cake, mix until just combined. The more you mix, the more domed your cake may get. This would mean having to trim more off the sponges, leaving you with a smaller cake.
- Roughly spread the buttercream for a rustic finish (I like to create little waves with the palette knife). Alternatively, to get your cake super smooth, place the scraper or palette knife in warm water for a few minutes before smoothing the buttercream.

CHOCOLATE FUDGE CAKE

A delicious, moist chocolate fudge cake made simple.
A go-to cake of mine that everyone adores.

SERVES 12
PREP TIME 2 HOURS 50
  MINS
COOK TIME 1 HOUR

Cake
150g dark chocolate
150g unsalted butter
150g plain flour
40g cocoa powder
1½ tsp baking powder
300g light brown sugar
pinch of salt
200ml buttermilk
3 eggs
**30ml espresso (or
  strong instant coffee)**

Ganache
300ml single cream
**300g dark chocolate,
  broken into pieces**

- Preheat the oven to 160°C/140°C fan/gas mark 3. Grease two 15cm (6 inch) cake tins and line each base with a circle of baking parchment.
- Melt the chocolate and butter in a bain-marie (see page 11) or the microwave and set aside to cool.
- Sift the flour, cocoa and baking powder into a bowl and add the sugar and salt.
- In a separate bowl, whisk together the buttermilk, eggs and espresso.
- Make a well in the dry ingredients and pour in both the wet mix and the chocolate mix and whisk until smooth, then divide the mixture evenly between the two tins.
- Bake for approximately 1 hour until a toothpick or skewer comes out clean. Cool in the tins for 15 minutes, then remove to a wire rack to cool completely.
- For the ganache, warm the cream over a low heat, then add the chocolate pieces. Stir until smooth and then refrigerate until it reaches a spreadable consistency (about two hours).
- Place one cake on a serving plate and add enough ganache for a smooth layer. Place the other cake on top and then cover all the cake with the remaining ganache.
- Finish with a palette knife. I like a textured finish but if you prefer a smooth finish, warm the palette knife in hot water before smoothing the ganache.
- This cake will keep for up to three days in an airtight container.

 GILL'S TIPS
Add the zest of two oranges, one to the cake and one to the ganache, for a deliciously rich chocolate orange cake.

BLACK FOREST CAKE

A long-standing family favourite, this rich, indulgent chocolate cake is soaked in cherry syrup and layered with a vanilla cream, jam and black cherries.

SERVES 12
PREP TIME 1 HOUR 50 MINS
COOK TIME 1 HOUR

Cake
150g dark chocolate
150g unsalted butter
150g plain flour
40g cocoa powder
1½ tsp baking powder
pinch of salt
300g light brown sugar
200ml buttermilk
30ml espresso (or
  strong instant coffee)
3 eggs
2 tsp almond extract

Syrup
40ml cherry syrup
  (from the tin of
  cherries – see extras)
20g caster sugar
1–2 tbsp kirsch
  (optional)

- Preheat the oven to 160°C/140°C fan/gas mark 3. Grease two 15cm (6 inch) cake tins and line each base with baking parchment.
- Melt the chocolate and butter in a bain-marie (see page 11) or the microwave and set aside to cool.
- Sift the flour, cocoa, baking powder and salt into a bowl. Add the sugar and stir.
- In a separate bowl, whisk together the buttermilk, espresso, eggs and almond extract.
- Make a well in the dry ingredients and pour in both the wet mix and chocolate mix and whisk until smooth. Divide the mixture evenly between the two tins and bake for approximately 1 hour until a toothpick or skewer comes out clean.
- Cool your cakes in the tin for 15 minutes, before removing to a wire rack to cool completely, and then slice each cake in two to give four layers.
- For the syrup, drain the tin of cherries into a bowl. Chop 100g cherries in half and set aside. Mix 40ml of the cherry liquid with the caster sugar (and the kirsch, if you like). Stir until the sugar dissolves.
- Next, put the cream and vanilla into a bowl, sift in the icing sugar, and whip (begin at a low speed or the sugar will fly everywhere).
- To assemble, place one of the cake layers on a serving plate and drizzle with a third of the syrup. Spread with a tablespoonful of jam and then add a layer of cream.

Cream

750ml double cream

1 tsp vanilla extract

60g icing sugar

Extras

100g tinned pitted cherries

85g raspberry or cherry jam

100g chocolate sprinkles

30g chocolate (dark or milk), melted

a handful of fresh (or tinned) cherries

- Scatter a third of the chopped cherries over the cream, and place another cake layer on top of the cherries. Repeat until the last cake is on top. Cover the whole cake with whipped cream and then cover with chocolate sprinkles.
- Pipe a ring of cream on the top of your cake. I like to make eight stars of cream and place some fresh (or tinned) cherries on top.
- Cover the centre of the cream with some extra jam and pipe some melted chocolate around the top rim of the cake so it drips down the edges.
- Decorate your cake however you prefer: I like to go with a classic Black Forest look.
- Slice and enjoy!
- This cake will keep for up to two days in the fridge.

 GILL'S TIPS

Decorating the sides of the cake with sprinkles can be tricky. Take a handful of sprinkles and gently press your palm into the sides, moving around the cake. This may take several goes to completely cover the cake. Do this over a clean countertop or a large bowl so that you can collect the fallen sprinkles to use again.

CARROT CAKE

* * *

A delicious spiced carrot cake base topped with a silky orange zest cream cheese frosting.
This super-soft cake is full of spice for a warm, creamy treat!

SERVES 12
PREP TIME 1 HOUR 15 MINS
COOK TIME 30–35 MINS

Cake
**140g vegetable/
    sunflower oil**
2 eggs
170g light brown sugar
zest of half an orange
200g self-raising flour
**1 tsp bicarbonate of
    soda/baking soda**
1 tsp ground cinnamon
1 tsp ground ginger
1 tsp mixed spice
½ tsp salt
**200g carrots, peeled
    and grated**
80g walnuts, chopped

Icing
225g unsalted butter
225g icing sugar
400g cream cheese
zest of half an orange

Decoration
a handful of walnuts
sprinkle of orange zest

- Preheat the oven to 180°C/160°C fan/gas mark 4. Grease and line two 15cm (6 inch) cake tins.
- Put the oil, eggs, sugar and orange zest in a mixing bowl and whisk. Sift in the flour, bicarbonate, spices and salt and fold. Add the carrots and walnuts and fold until combined.
- Spoon the mix into the cake tins and smooth down. Bake for 30–35 minutes until a toothpick or skewer comes out clean or the cakes spring back when pressed gently.
- Leave to cool completely before slicing each cake in two to give four layers.
- For the icing, cream the butter in a mixing bowl until pale and fluffy using an electric whisk. Sift in the icing sugar in two batches and whisk until fully combined (begin at a low speed or the sugar will fly everywhere).
- Next, whisk in the cream cheese and orange zest.
- Spread a small bit of icing on a serving plate and place one layer of cake on it. Pipe or spread about a quarter of the icing on top of the cake layer and then place the next cake layer on top. Repeat until you have used all four layers.
- Decorate the top of your cake however you prefer. I use walnuts and orange zest.
- This cake will keep for up to three days in an airtight container in the fridge.

 GILL'S TIPS
I usually decorate this as a lovely naked-cake style but if you want to completely cover the cake – top and sides – you will need to make more icing. Just multiply the icing ingredients by 1½ to get a good amount for covering.

CHOCOLATE ORANGE LOAF

A zesty rich chocolate cake covered in an outrageously orangey icing,
the perfect cake for a lover of orange chocolate!

SERVES 12
PREP TIME 2 HOURS 30
  MINS
COOK TIME 50–60 MINS

Cake
115g dark chocolate
115g unsalted butter
115g plain flour
30g cocoa powder
1 tsp baking powder
pinch of salt
225g light brown sugar
170ml buttermilk
2 eggs
zest of an orange
   (reserve a sprinkle
   for decoration)

Buttercream
40g dark chocolate,
   melted
100g unsalted butter,
   at room temperature
200g icing sugar
zest of an orange

- Preheat the oven to 180°C/160°C fan/gas mark 4. Grease a loaf tin and line the base with baking parchment.
- Melt the chocolate and butter in a bain-marie (see page 11) or a microwave and set aside to cool.
- Sift the flour, cocoa, baking powder and salt into a bowl, and add the sugar.
- In a separate bowl, whisk the buttermilk, eggs and orange zest.
- Make a well in the dry ingredients, pour in the wet mix and whisk until smooth. Spoon into the tin and bake for 50–60 minutes until a toothpick or skewer comes out clean. Cool for 15 minutes in the tin, then remove to a wire rack and allow it cool completely (about 2 hours).
- For the buttercream, melt the chocolate in a heatproof bowl in short blasts in the microwave, stirring regularly and set aside. Place the soft butter into a mixing bowl. Using an electric hand whisk, whip it until very pale and fluffy. This will take about five minutes. Sift in the icing sugar in two batches and whisk until incorporated well (begin at a low speed or the sugar will fly everywhere).
- Add the orange zest and melted chocolate and whisk again.
- Spread the buttercream on the top of the cake and decorate with some extra orange zest if you like!
- This will keep for up to three days in an airtight container.

GILL'S TIPS
Do you find it a pain to grease cake tins? Get yourself a non-stick spray and grease your tins in a matter of seconds.

STRAWBERRY SHORTCAKE

A delicious and super-easy strawberry shortcake-flavoured sponge, topped with luxurious whipped double cream and sweet syrupy strawberries. Summer heaven!

SERVES 8
PREP TIME 1 HOUR 45 MINS
COOK TIME 25–30 MINS

Cake
125g unsalted butter
125g caster sugar
1 tsp vanilla extract
2 eggs
125g self-raising flour
pinch of salt

Vanilla syrup
40ml water
40g caster sugar
1 tsp vanilla

Macerated strawberries
300g strawberries
30g caster sugar
1 tsp vanilla extract

Cream
250ml double cream
30g icing sugar
1 tsp vanilla extract

- Preheat the oven to 180°C/160°C fan/gas mark 4. Grease a 20cm (8 inch) round cake tin and line the base with baking parchment.
- In a mixing bowl, cream together the butter and sugar until pale and fluffy. Whisk in the vanilla. Next, whisk in eggs one at a time until combined. Sift the flour and salt into the mix and gently fold until just combined.
- Spoon the mix into the baking tin and spread evenly. Bake for 25–30 minutes until a toothpick or skewer comes out clean or the centre of the sponge springs back when pressed.
- Allow to cool on a wire rack for 10 minutes.
- Make the syrup by mixing all the ingredients together in a bowl. Poke the top of the cake with a toothpick or skewer multiple times (to allow the syrup to be absorbed evenly). Carefully spread with the vanilla syrup, using a pastry brush or spoon. Leave to cool completely (about an hour) and then place on a cake stand or plate.
- Slice the strawberries and mix in a bowl with the caster sugar and vanilla. Set aside for 10 minutes to get all syrupy.
- In a separate bowl, whip together the cream, icing sugar and vanilla until you have a thick, spreadable cream. Spoon this on top of the cooled cake. Layer on the syrupy strawberries.
- The cake can be made in advance but it's best eaten on the same day.

 GILL'S TIPS

For a two-layer cake, double the cake ingredients and bake in two cake tins. Double the syrup ingredients as well. This is the most delicious syrupy Victoria sponge-style cake and looks absolutely stunning too!

CHOCOLATE IRISH STOUT CAKE

A rich velvety stout and chocolate sponge topped with a smooth Irish cream icing.
You couldn't get more Irish or more indulgent!

SERVES 12
PREP TIME 1 HOUR 50 MINS
COOK TIME 70–85 MINS

Cake
150g dark chocolate,
** broken into pieces**
150g unsalted butter
150g plain flour
pinch of salt
40g cocoa powder
1½ tsp baking powder
300g light brown sugar
45ml buttermilk
85ml Irish stout
3 eggs
30ml espresso (or
** strong instant coffee)**

Icing
150g unsalted butter
300g icing sugar
40ml Irish cream
** liqueur**

Decoration (optional)
a sprig of fresh mint

- Preheat the oven to 160°C/140°C fan/gas mark 3. Grease a 20cm (8 inch) cake tin and line the base with baking parchment.
- In a heatproof bowl, melt the chocolate and butter together in short blasts in the microwave, stirring regularly, and then set aside to cool.
- Sift the flour, salt, cocoa and baking powder into a bowl, add the sugar and stir.
- In a separate bowl, whisk the buttermilk, stout, eggs and espresso.
- Make a well in the dry ingredients and pour in the wet mix and chocolate mix. Whisk until smooth. Spoon into the tin and bake for 70–85 minutes until a toothpick or skewer comes out clean.
- Allow to cool in the tin for 10–15 minutes and then remove to a wire rack to cool completely (about an hour and a half).
- While the cake is cooling, make the icing. Using an electric whisk, cream the butter until pale and fluffy. Sift in the icing sugar in two batches and whisk until fully combined (begin at a low speed or the sugar will fly everywhere).
- Add the liqueur and whisk again.
- Place the cake on a serving plate or cake stand and cover the top with icing, using a spatula or palette knife.
- Decorate however you prefer. I leave mine easy and textured, with a sprig of fresh mint as decoration.
- This cake will keep for up to three days in an airtight container.

 GILL'S TIPS
Don't want to use liqueur? Swap it for milk and a splash of vanilla extract.

LIME AND PASSION FRUIT LOAF

Looking for a sweet and zesty bake? This is the one for you! Packed full of fresh lime and zingy passion fruit, this cake will have your taste buds tingling for more!

SERVES 10
PREP TIME 1 HOUR 10 MINS
COOK TIME 50–60 MINS

Cake
225g unsalted butter
225g caster sugar
4 eggs
zest and juice of 2 limes
2 passion fruits (sieved for the juice)
225g self-raising flour
pinch of salt

Drizzle
2 limes, juiced
2 passion fruits (sieved for the juice)
100g caster sugar

Icing
150g icing sugar
2 tbsp lime juice

Decoration
zest of a lime
1 passion fruit

- Preheat the oven to 180°C/160°C fan/gas mark 4. Grease a loaf tin and line the base and sides with baking parchment.
- In a mixing bowl, cream together the butter and sugar until pale and fluffy. Crack in the eggs, one at a time, and whisk until combined. Mix in the zest and juice of two limes and the juice of two passion fruits.
- Sift in the flour and salt, and fold until combined.
- Spoon the mixture into the loaf tin and bake for 50–60 minutes until a toothpick or skewer comes out clean.
- Allow to cool for 15 minutes in the tin before adding the drizzle.
- For the drizzle, combine the lime juice and passion fruit juice with the sugar. Mix until the sugar dissolves. Poke plenty of holes in your cake with a skewer or toothpick and then drizzle with the mixture.
- Leave the cake to cool completely before placing it on the serving plate or cake stand.
- For the icing, combine the icing sugar and lime juice until smooth. Use more or less lime juice, depending on how runny you like your icing.
- Decorate the top of your cake with some lime zest and passion fruit.
- This cake will keep for up to three days in an airtight container.

 GILL'S TIPS
Make this cake a different flavour by simply swapping the passion fruit and limes for lemons (or oranges).

PISTACHIO AND RASPBERRY CAKE

My favouritest-ever combo of flavours! Pistachio is one of my favourite nuts and raspberry one of my favourite fruits so I had to bring them together for a showstopper stacked cake recipe. An explosion of flavour!

SERVES 12
PREP TIME 2–2½ HOURS
COOK TIME 32–40 MINS

Cake
225g unsalted butter
225g caster sugar
2 tsp almond extract
drop of green food gel (optional)
4 small eggs
125g self-raising flour
1 tsp baking powder
pinch of salt
100g pistachios (blitzed until fine)

Buttercream
400g unsalted butter, at room temperature
800g icing sugar
6 tbsp raspberry jam, sieved
1 tsp vanilla extract
2 tbsp crushed freeze-dried raspberries (optional)

- Preheat the oven to 180°C/160°C fan/gas mark 4. Grease two 15cm (6 inch) cake tins and line each base with a circle of baking parchment.
- In a mixing bowl, cream together the butter and sugar until pale and fluffy. Whisk in the almond extract and a drop of green food gel if using. Mix in the eggs, one at a time, until combined.
- Sift the flour, baking powder and salt into the mix, add the blitzed pistachios and gently fold.
- Divide the mixture evenly between the two baking tins.
- Bake for 32–40 minutes until a toothpick or skewer comes out clean or the centre of the sponges spring back when pressed. Allow them to cool in the tins for 10–15 minutes before removing to a wire rack.
- Once the cakes are completely cooled (about 90 minutes), trim a sliver off the top of each cake to make it flat, if necessary, then slice each cake horizontally in half to create four layers. (Tip: flip the upper layer of cake and use the base for a smoother top.)
- For the buttercream, place the soft butter into a mixing bowl. Using an electric whisk, whip it up until very pale and fluffy. This will take about 5 minutes. Sift in the icing sugar in 3 separate batches and whisk until incorporated well (begin at a low speed or the sugar will fly everywhere).
- Add the sieved jam and vanilla, and whisk until silky smooth. Pop in the freeze-dried raspberries now, if using them.

Decoration
75g pistachios, blitzed
100g fresh raspberries
small handful of
crushed freeze-dried
raspberries (optional)

- To assemble the cake, spread a small bit of buttercream on a serving board. Place one layer of cake on this. Pipe a ring of buttercream around the border of the top. Spread a tablespoonful of jam within the border, then top with some more buttercream. Place the next layer on top and repeat these steps until you get to the last layer. NB: Reserve about a third of the buttercream for icing the top and sides.
- Refrigerate the cake for about 20 minutes for the icing to firm up.
- Apply a very thin and smooth layer of buttercream all around the cake using a palette knife as a crumb coat. Place it back in the fridge for about 20 minutes until firm to touch.
- Now apply a thick coating of buttercream all around the cake. Using a cake scraper or a palette knife, smooth until you get a nice finish. You can finish this how you prefer, either going for a rustic finish or very smooth. Leave to set in the fridge for another 20 minutes.
- For decoration, take a handful of blitzed pistachios and gently press around the base of the cake. Pipe a ring of buttercream stars on top of the cake and pop a fresh raspberry on each star. Finish with an extra sprinkle of pistachios and freeze-dried raspberries (optional).
- Return to the fridge for at least 30 minutes before serving so you can get a good cut.
- This cake will keep for up to three days in the fridge.

 GILL'S TIPS

- Halve the amount of icing if you want a naked-style cake – still just as tasty!
- To get your final coating of buttercream super smooth on the cake, place the scraper or palette knife in warm water for a few minutes before using it.
- Sieving the jam to remove the seeds gives a lovely smooth texture to match the silky buttercream.

DESSERTS

BAKED CARAMEL CHEESECAKE

A smooth, creamy baked cheesecake with a buttery base, smothered in a homemade salted caramel.

SERVES 12
PREP TIME 5 HOURS 30 MINS
COOK TIME 45–50 MINS

Base
240g digestive biscuits
115g salted butter
pinch of cinnamon

Cheesecake
800g cream cheese
  (full fat)
100ml double cream
200g caster sugar
50g plain flour
3 eggs
zest of half a lemon
3 tsp vanilla extract

Caramel
250g caster sugar
225ml single cream
75g salted butter
pinch of salt

- Preheat the oven to 200°C/180°C fan/gas mark 6. Grease a 20cm (8 inch) springform tin and line the base with baking parchment.
- Crush the digestives to a fine crumb (either in a food processor or bash them in a bowl or Ziploc bag with a rolling pin). Melt the butter and add it to the crumbs, mixing until combined. Mix in a pinch of cinnamon. Press the mixture into the tin and place in the freezer for 10–15 minutes until solid.
- While the base is setting, put all the cheesecake ingredients into a large mixing bowl. Mix until everything is well combined. Pour on top of the biscuit base and smooth over until level.
- Bake for 45–50 minutes until the sides are well set and the centre still has a slight wobble. Leave to cool in the oven with the door slightly open for 30 minutes, then cool at room temperature for about an hour and then place in the fridge until completely cold (this will take about 4 hours).
- To make the caramel, put the sugar into a saucepan over a medium heat (don't stir, as this may make the sugar stick to the sides of the saucepan where it will crystallise). Cook until the sugar has melted and turned an amber colour.
- Remove from the heat and whisk in the cream. Add the butter and mix until melted. Pour the caramel into a clean bowl and leave to cool at room temperature.
- Finally, pour the cooled caramel over the cheesecake and serve.
- This will keep for up to three days in the fridge.

 GILL'S TIPS
Looking to save time? Use a shop-bought caramel instead.

CHOCOLATE FONDANT PUDDINGS

A rich chocolate pudding baked to gooey perfection.
One of my go-to desserts for a sweet extra-chocolatey kick!

SERVES 2
PREP TIME 20 MINS
COOK TIME 12–14 MINS

1 tbsp melted butter,
  for greasing
1 tbsp cocoa powder,
  for dusting
60g salted butter
60g dark chocolate,
  broken into pieces
60g caster sugar
1 egg
1 egg yolk
½ tsp vanilla extract
20g plain flour
5g cocoa powder

- Preheat the oven to 200°C/180°C fan/gas mark 6. Grease two pudding bowls or moulds with melted butter, then lightly coat the insides with cocoa powder.
- In a heatproof bowl, melt the butter and chocolate in the microwave in short blasts, stirring regularly until smooth. (This will take 1–2 minutes.) Leave to cool for about 10 minutes.
- In a separate bowl, whisk the sugar, eggs and vanilla until light and fluffy. Stir in the chocolate/butter mixture.
- Sift in the flour and cocoa powder, and fold until incorporated. Pour the mixture into the moulds and bake for 12–14 minutes. Leave to rest for 5 minutes.
- Using a cloth, tip each mould onto a serving plate. Dust with some icing sugar and serve immediately.

GILL'S TIPS

- This makes two servings but you can multiply the recipe for as many servings as you need.
- You can make these in advance by placing the filled moulds in the fridge and when it's time to bake, add an extra 3–4 minutes to the cooking time.

STICKY TOFFEE PUDDING

A sticky spiced sponge covered in a rich and gooey toffee sauce and vanilla ice cream.
A dessert you just cannot beat!

SERVES 4
PREP TIME 30 MINS
COOK TIME 25 MINS

Cake
80g pitted dates,
roughly chopped
¼ tsp bicarbonate of
soda/baking soda
60ml hot water
2 tbps treacle
45g unsalted butter, at
room temperature
80g dark brown sugar
1 tsp vanilla extract
1 small egg
100g self-raising flour
pinch of salt
⅛ tsp ground cinnamon
⅛ tsp ground ginger
40g pecans, roughly
chopped

Toffee sauce
60g salted butter
120g brown sugar
1 tsp treacle
30ml single cream

To serve
ice cream

- Preheat the oven to 180°C/160°C fan/gas mark 4. Grease four pudding moulds.
- Put the dates, bicarbonate of soda and hot water into a bowl and soak for 10–15 minutes, and then blend in a food processor or break down with a fork, keeping the water in it. Mix in the treacle and then set aside.
- In a mixing bowl, cream together the butter and sugar until pale and fluffy. Whisk in the vanilla. Crack in the egg and mix until combined. Next, whisk in the blended date mix.
- Sift in the flour, salt and spices, add the chopped pecans and fold until just combined.
- Spoon the mixture into the pudding moulds and smooth down flat. Bake for approximately 25 minutes, until a toothpick or skewer comes out clean.
- While your puddings are baking, put all the toffee sauce ingredients into a medium saucepan over a medium heat. Bring to a boil while stirring continually. Cook until the sugar has completely dissolved (this will take 2 to 4 minutes). Set aside for serving.
- When the puddings are baked, leave them to cool for about five minutes before carefully turning them upside down onto the serving plates.
- Top with a scoop of ice cream, drizzle on the toffee sauce and tuck in while they're warm.

 GILL'S TIPS
You can make these in advance and warm them in the microwave just before adding your toppings and serving.

CARAMEL AND CHOCOLATE ICE-CREAM CAKE

A childhood favourite of mine. This Viennetta-style dessert brings me right back to being a kid at my friends' birthday parties. This version is just insanely good!

SERVES 12
PREP TIME 6 HOURS 30 MINS

550ml double cream
200ml condensed milk
2 tsp vanilla extract
250g milk chocolate, melted
397g tin caramel or dulce de leche

- Line a 900g (2 lb) loaf tin completely with cling film, leaving extra over the sides so you can easily lift out your ice cream.
- For the ice-cream mix, in a large bowl, whisk the double cream, condensed milk and vanilla until very thick.
- Melt the chocolate either in a heatproof bowl in the microwave in short bursts or in a bain-marie (see page 11).
- Spoon in enough of the ice-cream mix to cover the base of the loaf tin.
- Drizzle with a layer of caramel and then a layer of melted chocolate.
- Top with more of the ice-cream mix.
- Repeat these steps until you have used up all the ingredients. Place in the freezer to set for at least 6 hours or overnight.
- Invert a serving plate onto the loaf tin and then flip both upside down. Lift off the loaf tin and peel off the cling film.
- Drizzle with some extra melted chocolate and caramel for decoration, if you like.
- Any leftovers should be kept in the freezer.

 GILL'S TIPS
Change this up with other flavours you like! Add some cocoa powder to the base mix for an extra chocolate boost.

BANOFFEE PIE

Buttery biscuit base, thick dulce de leche, sliced banana, sweet vanilla cream and chocolate flakes. A classic that never disappoints!

SERVES 12
PREP TIME 30 MINS

250g biscuits (digestives or Biscoff), crushed

150g unsalted butter

397g tin dulce de leche or caramel

3 bananas, sliced to 5mm thick

25g icing sugar

350ml double cream

1 tsp vanilla extract

50g chocolate, grated

- Grease a 20cm (8 inch) tart/pie tin.
- Crush the biscuits to a fine crumb in a food processor, or in a bowl or Ziploc bag using a rolling pin.
- In a saucepan over a medium heat, melt the butter, add it to the crumbs and stir until combined.
- Press the mixture into the tin and place in the freezer for about 15 minutes until solid.
- Once solid, pour the dulce de leche/caramel onto the crumb base. Top with slices of banana.
- Sift the icing sugar into a bowl, add the double cream and vanilla and whisk with an electric whisk. Begin at a low speed or the sugar will fly everywhere, and then increase the speed and whisk until you have thick, stiff peaks.
- Spoon over the bananas.
- Garnish with grated chocolate and serve straight away or place in the fridge until needed.

GILL'S TIPS
Make these into mini individual tarts using small tart tins.

SUMMER FRUIT PAVLOVA

A crisp, light meringue with a pillowy marshmallow centre, topped with a sweet vanilla cream and piled high with fresh fruit.

SERVES 12
PREP TIME 2 HOURS
COOK TIME 90 MINS

Meringue
6 egg whites
300g caster sugar
1 tsp white vinegar
2 tsp cornflour

Vanilla cream
600ml double cream
50g icing sugar
1 tsp vanilla extract

75g berry coulis
300g approx. fresh berries/fruit (sliced raspberries, blueberries, blackberries and strawberries)
a couple of sprigs of mint, for decoration (optional)

- Preheat the oven to 150°C/130°C fan/gas mark 2.
- Lay a sheet of baking parchment on a baking tray and draw a 20cm (8 inch) diameter circle on it (use a cake tin). This will be your guide for the meringue. Flip the sheet so that it doesn't mark the meringue.
- Put the egg whites in a large bowl and, using an electric whisk, beat until you have soft peaks. Add the caster sugar a tablespoonful at a time until it is all incorporated and you have stiff glossy peaks.
- Whisk in the vinegar and cornflour until just combined.
- Spoon the meringue into an even round disc on the baking parchment, using the circle as your guide. Build the sides up higher than the centre.
- Bake for about 90 minutes until the outside is crisp.
- Switch off the oven but leave the meringue inside with the oven door shut. Leave it to cool in the oven for about 30 minutes, then remove to a wire rack to cool completely (a further 30 minutes). This is your time to prep the fruit.
- Pour the cream into a bowl, sift in the icing sugar, add the vanilla and whisk until thickened.
- To assemble, carefully place the meringue on a serving plate. Spoon all the cream on top, drizzle with some coulis and layer with the fruit. Decorate with some mint sprigs (optional) and serve.

 GILL'S TIPS
Make this recipe into mini individual pavlovas or even an Eton mess (break the baked meringue into pieces, then mix in the cream, sliced berries and coulis and serve in pretty glasses).

LUXURIOUS BREAD AND BUTTER PUDDING

Bread and butter pudding is a hug in a bowl. A warm custard-soaked brioche dotted with melted chocolate and with a zesty orange kick. I love this on a cold day with a big cup of tea!

SERVES 6
PREP TIME 20 MINS
COOK TIME 30 MINS

30g salted butter, softened
200g brioche bread
75g milk chocolate chips
200ml double cream
150g milk
2 eggs
40g caster sugar
zest of an orange
30g brown sugar

To serve
pouring cream or ice cream

- Grease a medium-sized baking dish with all the softened butter.
- Cut the brioche into chunks and place them in the dish. Scatter with chocolate chips.
- In a separate bowl, whisk together the cream, milk, eggs, caster sugar and orange zest. Pour this mixture over the bread and leave it to soak for about 15 minutes.
- Preheat the oven to 200°C/180°C fan/gas mark 6.
- Sprinkle the brown sugar over the pudding and bake for about 30 minutes until golden brown on top.
- Serve straight away with some extra pouring cream or ice cream.

 GILL'S TIPS
Not a fan of chocolate or orange? Replace them with raspberries, apples, dried fruit or nuts.

CRÈME BRÛLÉE TART

A mix of two classic desserts made into a delicious creamy, caramelised tart!

SERVES 12
PREP TIME 60 MINS
COOK TIME 65–75 MINS

Pastry
250g plain flour
1 tsp caster sugar
100g salted butter, cold and cubed
4–5 tbsp cold water
egg wash (see Gill's Tips)

Custard filling
350ml double cream
2 tsp vanilla extract
75g caster sugar
4 egg yolks

Extra
4 tbsp caster sugar

- Grease a 20cm (8 inch) tart tin.
- Sift the flour into a mixing bowl, add the sugar and stir. Add the chopped-up butter and rub it in with your fingertips until you get the texture of fine breadcrumbs. Mix in the water until you have a soft dough.
- Place the dough on a floured surface, and roll out into a circle slightly bigger than your dish and about 5 mm thick. Make sure to keep the surface and rolling pin floured to prevent the pastry sticking.
- Line the tin with the pastry – drape it over the rolling pin to lift it. Try to get it as neat and even as possible. Shave off excess pastry around the edges (use your thumb or a knife). Chill in the fridge for 25–30 minutes.
- Preheat the oven to 200°C/180°C fan/gas mark 6.
- Once the pastry has chilled, crumple up some baking parchment and open it back up. Place it on top of the pastry and fill with baking beans/rice/dried peas. (This help keeps the tart base from puffing up as it bakes.)
- Bake in the oven for 20–25 minutes. Remove from the oven, take out the baking beans and parchment and return to the oven for about 10 minutes until the crust is fully baked: it will be lightly browned and firm.
- Remove the tart from the oven, brush with egg wash and return it to the oven for 5 more minutes. Leave to cool on a wire rack.
- Keep the oven on while you make the custard filling: put the cream and vanilla into a medium saucepan over a medium heat until warm.

- In a separate bowl, whisk the egg yolks and sugar together. When the cream is warm, slowly pour it into the egg mix, stirring continually. Pour the mixture back into the saucepan and cook until slightly thickened, stirring all the time (about five minutes). You'll know it's cooked when you can draw a clean line with your finger through the custard on the back of a spoon.
- Pour the custard into your tart base. Bake for 30–35 minutes until there's only a very slight jiggle in the centre. Allow it to cool on a wire rack and then put it in the fridge to set.
- When serving, sprinkle the top of your tart with caster sugar. Using a blowtorch or a medium grill, melt the sugar until amber in colour all over.
- Slice up and serve!

 GILL'S TIPS
- Add some zest or spices to the custard for an extra dimension of flavour, e.g. ½ tsp cinnamon, ground cloves or orange zest.
- Use one or two of the egg whites from the separated eggs, beaten, as a wash for the pastry.

INDEX